350

HUSSEIN OF JORDAN

His Majesty King Hussein, G.C.V.O.
By courtesy of Studio Angelo

HUSSEIN OF JORDAN

by

GERALD SPARROW

with twenty-one illustrations in half-tone

GEORGE G. HARRAP & CO. LTD
LONDON TORONTO WELLINGTON SYDNEY

First published in Great Britain 1960
by GEORGE G. HARRAP & CO. LTD
182 High Holborn, London, W.C.1

© *Gerald Sparrow* 1960

Composed in Baskerville type and printed by
Jarrold & Sons Ltd, Norwich
Made in Great Britain

TO

HIS MAJESTY KING HUSSEIN, G.C.V.O.

in appreciation of the unique facilities
granted by him to the author,
both in Jordan and in Britain,
and in grateful acknowledgment
of his personal interest and encouragement

Preface

On my last visit to Jordan I asked King Hussein if I might write this book, and he gave me permission to do so. He went much farther than this, affording me unique opportunities for seeing all Jordan, while his amiable and able photographer, Mr Fluti, provided me with all the photographs I needed.

It was the King's courage that made me want to write this book and, I hope, may make you wish to read it. Whatever his faults may be as a man, or a King, his courage and determination are unquestioned even by his enemies. When Richard Dimbleby, on a brilliant B.B.C. programme, asked the King, "Do you not, sir, fear for your person?" the King's reply, "No, sir. I fear no one but God," sounded what it was—a simple statement of fact.

I have tried to observe two rules in painting this portrait of the King. He is only twenty-five, and I have attempted to describe him in terms of what he is doing rather than in terms of what he is. This book does not pretend to be a 'life'—the King's life has only just begun.

The second rule I have adopted is to tell the story, in so far as I am able, looking out on the world from Amman or Jerusalem, rather than looking in on Jordan from Paris, Washington, or London. I think this question of point of view very important. When the B.B.C. asked me to supply material for a television programme indicating the keys to the King's character and behaviour

I replied that they were twofold; first, that he was the last surviving ruling member of the Hashemite House, and a grandson of the great Emir Abdullah; and, secondly, that the King was a Moslem Prince, a direct descendant of the Prophet, with the sense of mission which that lineage gives him.

It always surprises me that in Britain we expect new nations to be able to adopt the democratic form of government overnight. It took at least three centuries to win our limited form of political democracy in Britain. Jordan is not yet a full democracy, but it is at least as democratic as President Nasser's regime, and a great deal more democratic than General Quassem's thinly veiled quasi-Communist regime, with its ghoulish mass political trials.

In order to establish true democracy in Jordan there must be a united State of Jordan. Until recently the Kingdom was very divided. The union of a part of Palestine with Transjordan, of the Palestinian Arabs with the bedouin, could not be realized quickly. This, during the past five years, has been the major problem which the King has had to tackle. Unity has been his one primary objective. To a great extent he has achieved it.

As Hussein enters the decade of the sixties the real test comes. If he is content to have achieved unity, and to rely on a modified form of absolutism, he will still be remembered for his bravery and his leadership; but if, as I believe, he now intends to make Jordan a modern democratic and constitutional monarchy, he may well emerge as one of the great Arab leaders of our time.

I may well be told that I present the King in too favourable a light. Denigration is fashionable and popular. I have in fact written of the King exactly as he appeared to me to be. I hold the view that a very remarkable young man has stepped on to the world stage, a young man first and foremost an Arab and a Jordanian. But, because by instinct, judgment, and tradition he is friendly to the West, we should welcome him, for if we do not welcome our friends we may well have to compromise with our enemies.

It is because I believe that Hussein and what he stands for are of major importance that I found this book exciting to write, and I hope that this may have resulted in a book that will interest a great many people.

GERALD SPARROW

BLACKHEATH, 1960

Contents

Contents

Illustrations

I

Portrait of a Young King

The modern world tends to be dominated by elderly personalities past their prime. The era of Winston Churchill is only just over, and President Eisenhower, Dr Adenauer, and General de Gaulle are still in control of great affairs.

The explanation is simple. We are all afraid. The menace of the mushroom cloud is never absent from our minds. In the desperate situation in which we find ourselves it is natural that we should cling to the statesmen whom we know, and who, in the past, have served us well.

Yet, in fourteen years, our elderly leaders have been unable to rid us of the aftermath of the last war, while they do not yet seem to have achieved much success in preventing the next war, perhaps the last war.

It is with relief that we can welcome a young leader playing a minor, but vital, rôle.

Vital, young, with the high hope of youth, Hussein of Jordan, in five short years, has sprung into the centre of the international stage, and the elderly actors pause for a moment in the wings to take a searching look at this confident young man.

It was on November 14, 1935, that His Royal Highness, Prince Talal, Heir Apparent to King Abdullah, had a son by his wife, the Princess Zayn, in the Royal Palace of

Raghadan, in Amman. The boy was called Hussein, a name honoured and loved in the history of the Hashemite House. The child was small, bright-eyed, very quick in his responses. People interested in astrology noted that he had been born under the sign of Scorpio, one of the most brilliant constellations of the Zodiac. The Eastern scorpion has eight eyes and a lethal sting; it is equally quick in attack and defence. In the city of Amman prayers were offered in the mosques, prayers of thanksgiving for the birth of the Prince.

In from the desert rode the bedouin chiefs, the sheikhs and their men to offer their congratulations. The Raghadan Palace, built of that same stone that is hewed from the quarries of Amman, seethed with bustle and excitement. Prince Talal held that type of open court so typical of Arabia. All his men would come and go without ceremony, for, though regard for the Hashemite House was high, the bedouin has always retained his own dignity and freedom.

The townspeople too in Amman and from Jerusalem sent gifts to the Palace—work in gold, in mother-of-pearl, and in silver. Hussein started with every advantage. There was as yet no hint of the terrible events that were to make his path a very rough and dangerous one.

In order to understand the events, often turbulent, of King Hussein's reign, it is necessary to know how the Kingdom of Jordan came into being.

After the break-up of the Ottoman Empire Britain administered a mandate for Palestine. It was a firm, enlightened rule of absolute justice, but, of course, it was a mandate to rule and administer without popular approval or support. It was in no way democratic. It did not pretend to be. The security and stable conditions it provided brought prosperity to the Palestinian Arabs for the first time in four hundred years. For the first time too the windows of Western culture, as well as the tendrils of trade, were opened to Palestinians. They became part of Western society. The long black-out of Turkish rule was over.

Transjordan did not come within the mandate. It was ruled by Abdullah, as Emir, in the closest collaboration with the British. It remained feudal, Arab or bedouin, adhering to the old ways while Palestine forged ahead.

At midnight on May 14, 1948, Britain terminated her Palestine mandate, and withdrew her troops. The fighting that broke out between Arabs and Jews was halted by an Armistice Agreement signed on April 3, 1949, Dr Ralph Bunche acting as mediator. Immediately British troops left Palestine the Jewish National Council proclaimed the foundation of the new State of Israel. King Abdullah was proclaimed King of United Transjordan and Palestine in December 1948. A boundary was fixed to divide his territories from 'Jewish-occupied territory.' The King gave a new name to his new kingdom —The Hashemite Kingdom of Jordan.

King Abdullah ruled his State of Jordan with a firm hand. No one said No to the King. He was a patriarch, feared and respected in the Arab tradition. His assassination while he was at prayer in the Mosque of the Rock, in Jerusalem, angered the entire nation. It was as insane and awful a crime as the murder of Mahatma Gandhi. The King's son, the Crown Prince Talal, came to the throne. As early as 1950 he showed signs of deep mental instability, and by 1953, no longer able to rule, he was moved to a home in Turkey. Thus, before his time, while still at school at Harrow, the young Hussein was proclaimed King.

It was an amazing turn of events for a boy still at school. It opened up, as an immediate prospect, the turbulent, sometimes treacherous, life of Eastern politics that seemed so remote at the school on the hill. Hussein took his fate, as he took everything else, with apparent calm. At Harrow he left two impressions behind him. His housemaster said of him, "He had an innate dignity beyond his years. One would almost have thought that he was already concerned with his destiny. But he entered into every activity with zest, determined to be at least as good as the next man."

This impression was confirmed at Sandhurst. It was decided in Amman that as the King was under age he should attend the Royal Military Academy for a shortened course, and the commandant permitted the young King to take the full course compressed into six months, including the final examinations and passing out. I spoke to many of those who had been responsible for the King's career at Sandhurst, not only to his commanding officer, but to Regimental Sergeant-Major Lord, who drilled the King. By this time the young man had grown in stature. His quiet self-reliance and confidence, though modestly borne, was pronounced. Every man I spoke to commented on this feature of the King's personality, and R.S.M. Lord added one comment of his own—"He took drilling and discipline very well. Perhaps that is why he has been able to discipline others during the last few years."

The halcyon days ended. On May 2, 1954, the King

opened the Jordanian Parliament in Amman, his first exercise in constitutional power. The people saw their King, a boy no longer, in a new light. This slim, vital man, with the firm, intent gaze, had the peculiar, un-analysed quality of kingship. The Arabs recognized this instantly. New hope came to Jordan. Under a new king, and a young one, it was felt that the nation would move forward, taking its place among the Arab states as an acknowledged Power, independent and fearless.

The King was small of stature, but his people remarked that he was not like any one else. His personality, what-ever it might be and however it might develop, was unique. Surrounded by other Jordanians, whether dressed in European clothes or in the 'kafear' and Arab robes, no one, for a moment, doubted who was the King.

Once more it was a high day and a holiday in Amman. The Arab Legion, under the command of the legendary Glubb Pasha, was on parade. Ministers surrounded the King, who now began to collect a personal entourage, in the manner of Eastern rulers. The entourage were watched by the politicians, and the politicians were observed by the entourage.

The great sheikhs of the Beni Sakhr bedouin[1] rode into Amman to give their allegiance to the young King. The narrow, dusty streets of Amman seethed with excitement. The King, who seemed tireless, spoke to each man in turn. In the autocracy of the East there has always been a personal democracy founded on the dignity of a man. Approach to the ruler in person is a very old

[1] The Beni Sakhr bedouin provide a large proportion of the recruitment of the modern Jordan Army.

tradition. The King was Hussein, their man, and they came to salute him as such.

His name became a part of the Arab legend that centres round the names of their leaders—Mohammed, Faisal, Abdullah.

There is no doubt that at this time the King's mother, Queen Zayn, a woman of strong personality and considerable beauty, exercised influence over her son. He was devoted to her; he still is; but within two years the King was making all his own decisions, with the advice of his Ministers. He matured very quickly—perhaps too quickly—in the forcing-house of Jordanian affairs.

What were the influences that had formed the King's character up to his manhood? It is very easy to exaggerate the importance of his foreign education. The influence of his grandfather, King Abdullah, probably weighed more heavily with the young Hussein. It was Abdullah who taught Hussein the passages from the Koran that led to his unswerving trust in God, and it was Abdullah who told him the long and eventful story of the Sharifian family of Mecca, descended directly from the Prophet, Mohammed. Hussein soon knew that among his near ancestors were such great figures as Hussein, King of the Hejaz from 1916 to 1924; Faisal, the first King of Syria and later the founder of modern Iraq; Abdullah himself, the man now teaching him, full of years and wisdom, Emir of Transjordan, then the first King of this Hashemite House.

These men had ridden with Lawrence and his men. They had seen the war-time leadership and cunning of Britain defeat and overthrow the mighty Ottoman Empire, exploiting its weaknesses and using the resurgent

Arab revolution as a weapon of war. These men too had seen the new nations rise out of the dust of battle—Syria, Iraq, Israel, Jordan, Egypt, the Lebanon; and now these peoples had become political states resolving their own destiny.

News of the cowardly and vile murder of his cousin, King Faisal of Iraq, came as a sudden shock of horror to King Hussein. It was understandable that the Iraq Army might wish to usurp the power exercised for so long by the tough, wily Nuri Said, who achieved much for Iraq, but that they should murder their young King, and desecrate the Koran in doing so, was, to Hussein, almost unbelievable.

The Arab Union of Jordan and Iraq had only recently become a reality. They were now one nation, linked for mutual support and strength. Together Jordan and Iraq were the strongest Middle East unit—stronger than Nasser's United Arab Republic.

The Arab Union into which the two young kings had solemnly entered was a real union of genuinely Arab peoples. They had abolished all the artificial barriers that divided their nations, customs, political frontiers, dual parliaments. They had joined hands in brotherhood and looked forward eagerly to working together. Everywhere in Amman one saw the portrait of the gentle, handsome young Faisal. One still does, for the Jordanians were disgusted by the murder of the young King of Iraq, and still revere his memory.

Hussein, learning in a hard school, grew steadily in stature. He increased his influence with the Jordan Army. He sealed off his border with Iraq. The flag flew at half-mast on the new Basman Palace. But there was no panic, no surrender. The Jordan people and their King had been grievously wounded, but, with the courage of their race, they faced the future, whatever it might hold, with absolute determination.

Hussein, from his earliest days, has been brought up as an Arab prince. At five he attended a kindergarten school in Amman. At eight we find him at Victoria College in Cairo. At fourteen he is at Harrow, and then, finally, comes the short, intensive course at Sandhurst. The background may appear foreign, yet it was not. His advisers were always his own people. Unlike some Arab rulers, he never had foreigners in his inner circle of friends and acquaintances, unless we count the Royal Air Force officers who helped him to become a first-class Hunter jet pilot.

He remained true to his faith, absolutely. He was a son of the Prophet, and still is. Whether he is sleeping in the Raghadan Palace, Amman, or in the Dorchester Hotel, London, Hussein turns to Mecca for his strength and courage. And the Prophet has given fortitude to his son.

Hussein has now won a place in the affections of the American and British peoples, who like a young man who is brave and 'sticks to his guns.' But in order to know Hussein, it is necessary to go to Jordan and see him as he is and as he rules.

You must go there by air, for there is no other way these days.

Comet or Caravelle take only five hours to reach Beirut —the capital of the Lebanon—where the white snow mountains come almost down to the sapphire-blue of the sea; a gracious town, with Arab dignity and French manners. From Beirut another plane will take you to

King Hussein, Samir Rifai, and the representative of the American Phillips Oil Company when the first refinery well was started in Jordan

By courtesy of Studio Angelo

22

King Hussein and Samir Rifai greet a foreign guest at a banquet in the royal palace

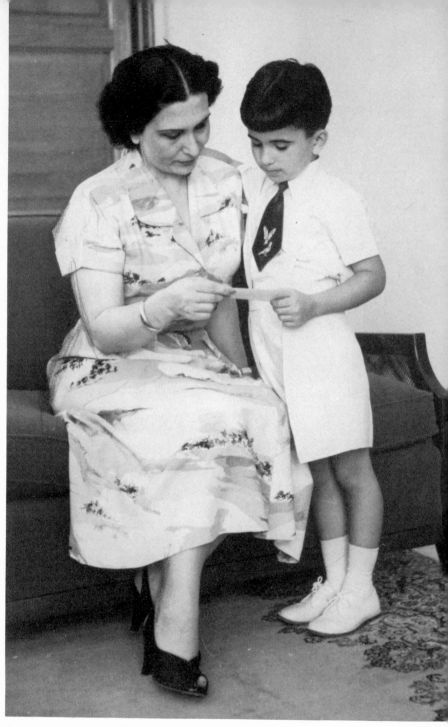

Queen Mother Zayn teaching Prince Hassan
By courtesy of Studio Angelo

Amman, via Jerusalem. There is one curious political detail here. Passports must not have on them any Israeli visas or notes; for the State of Israel is not recognized by Jordan. It is still 'Jewish-occupied territory.'

It is a short, hazardous flight through the mountains to Jerusalem, and then less than half an hour north to Amman. I visited Amman very recently, intending to stay only a few days. I stayed many weeks, and this was due entirely to the kindness of the King. There is this phenomenon in Jordan: until you have met the King and he has approved of you, very little can be accomplished. Ministers will be polite—and disinterested. They will make you welcome, and that is all. But when the King has given you the accolade of his friendship all doors open. For the people trust the judgment of their King. Then you know what Jordanian hospitality can be like.

From this moment you may see, in the most favourable circumstances, the secret ruins of Petra, the temple of Herod, the Roman city of Jerash, the vast civilian camps for the half million Arab refugees, the headquarters of the Jordan Army, the Camel Corps, the palace of the King himself, the life of the markets, the black tents of the bedouin. Everywhere you will be greeted by one word— "Welcome!"

It is a great experience. And then you become aware of something else. You get to know that the nerve-centre of this dynamic, romantic country is not the office of the Ministers, but the palace of the King on the hill, the Basman Palace, on Jebel Amman—an unpretentious building, long and low, cool, and clear in the Jordanian sun. The telephone to the palace is the link to all that goes on in Jordan. The steps taken to defeat a drought, a visit from the Secretary-General of U.N.O., the arrest of a politician said to be plotting against the regime, a visit by the King to his Arab Legion—all these activities centre round the palace. Visiting reporters know this, and the telephone to the palace is busy from morning until late at night.

The King sleeps late but is tireless in his duties. On visiting days the Basman Palace is thronged with his people from near and far—farmers from the Jordan valley who need more water, bedouin who are building a school, his own Ministers, who have their departmental cares : all are received by the King, unhurried, with time to spare.

Foreigners are usually received in the King's working study with a Minister present, but the King received me on several occasions in this small room alone. I had the opportunity of studying him as he is to-day, without an entourage, without a dictaphone, without the Press, before whom his responses would have to be careful. And now I think I know the key to his character, his impact.

Hussein has charm. He is very quiet in repose, but the lively brown eyes regard you with animation. He is quick and clear in his thinking, cutting through a conversation to the core of the matter under discussion. During one interview, for example, I asked him whether the American Phillips Company still had a chance of discovering oil in Jordan. Immediately he was on the *qui vive*.

"Why, yes, indeed they have. They have failed three times. It may be a question of four times lucky! That would alter our whole position. Our reliance on loans would go overnight. We could afford to finance the projects that the Jordanian farmers need so urgently. It would be a great blessing for us."

As he spoke I tried to determine who it was to whom I was really speaking—the Sandhurst cadet, the old Harrovian, the young Prince enjoying the first taste of power? The answer was, it was none of these. I was talking to a man with the enthusiasm of youth, but who had already matured before his age, in the hard school of Eastern politics.

He came to the throne at the beginning of the Near-Eastern crisis. He saw King Farouk exiled, the gentle Faisal murdered. President Nasser shot like a white star into the Eastern firmament, and in Baghdad the Red Star of General Quassem shone in defiance. Hussein, they said, was doomed. It was only a matter of weeks. But the King held on with grim determination. He refused to be panicked. His mission, he said, had only just begun.

I was talking to an Arab leader. There was no doubt of it. When the world was young the young men often ruled. Hannibal had crossed the Alps at twenty-six. Young men in power, young men ruling, were accepted as part of life. They had the high courage of youth. They were undaunted.

Hussein has become an adult and responsible Arab leader, and the leader of the Jordanian people in the white-hot crucible of modern Eastern affairs.

I noticed that as he talked he invariably took the line, What will this mean to Jordan? How will it benefit the Jordanians? His people were his responsibility. After four hundred years of Ottoman domination and a quarter of a century of Anglo-French rule, the Arab states were again emerging to manhood. What kind of renaissance was this to be? Were the great days of Arab glory to be revived? days when their Empire stretched from Russia, through Arabia, along Africa, through Spain to France? Was this a major convulsion of history? or was it merely the growth to nationhood of some new, strategically important states in the Near and Middle East?

I knew as I spoke to Hussein, and learnt more and more about him, that here was a man whose heart belonged to his own people. This was the secret of his success. I had the impression that he was determined to preserve and develop Jordan as a nation no matter what the difficulties might be. How he was to achieve this I do not think he had fully worked out.

He seemed to me to be concerned with survival, and if a strong hand was necessary a strong hand there would be. Treachery would be avenged. But how was he to bring a broad, stable democratic foundation to his kingdom? That he had not fully grappled with. It is on his ability to do just this that his name and fame will rest.

2

The King at Work

Very few people in Amman work after noon. Offices, both business and Government, usually close at midday. Only the King works from morning till night. This is one of the first things one notices after a few days in Amman.

King Hussein works in his Basman Palace, a building guarded by Jordanian soldiers wearing the red-and-white checked 'kafear' of the Jordan Army; but he often sleeps in the Raghadan Palace of his mother, Queen Zayn. The King loves his family, and spends his spare time—which gets less and less—with his mother, brothers, and his small daughter. They are an unusual Royal family, for they are all so young, but Hussein has now become their established and acknowledged head.

To-day Queen Zayn is still a beautiful woman, looking much younger than she is. It is difficult to believe she is the King's mother. Proud and—in Jordan—strictly orthodox, she is a woman of character and intelligence. The daughter of a former Court Chamberlain, Sharif Jamil Nasir, she is looked up to, and consulted by, the whole family, including the King. But the King makes his political decisions with his Ministers, keeping these separate from his family affairs.

Hussein's eldest brother, the Crown Prince Moham-med, is devoted to his brother, the King. A report published in the European Press that Hussein had temporarily exiled Mohammed was so patently untrue that the King laughed at it. But it hurt Mohammed very much, for loyalty is almost a fetish within this family. It has to be.

The younger brother, Prince Hassan, at school in England, is a boy of unusual aptitude—independent, reliable, a schoolboy's mischief shining through his dignity. Once I travelled in the same plane as Hassan. He was, technically, in the charge of an English governess. Leaving Amman in a dust-storm—the King was there, hatless on the 'Tarmac,' to see his brother off—Hassan inspected the Police guard of honour with a composure and discipline that won him the approval of the men lined up in his honour. At Jerusalem it was raining, monsoon rain that came down in a silver sheet. An official boarded the plane. The dignitaries had come to the airport to meet their Prince. Should they come aboard as it was raining so hard?

"No, I'll come," said Hassan, and, under a huge umbrella, the small boy marched to the airport lounge, carrying out his duties as if Royal receptions were just part and parcel of his school life.

The Palace is enlivened by two little girls—the Princess Basma, Hussein's youngest sister; and his own daughter by the former Queen Dinah, the Princess Aliya —Queen Zayn's grandchild. This makes a family circle where no one is ever lonely and few are unhappy except fleetingly. This circle forms the background of Hussein's life, the charmed company of very young people who love him, and whom he loves.

The King himself is in some ways the antithesis of traditional Arab monarchy. He is athletic and quick, a jet pilot who could have qualified as a racing motorist, so good is his nerve, so swift his responses. To his people, he seems a Prince of the Space Age; but they know—the bedouin Arabs as well as the Palestinians—that under all this Hussein cherishes his faith and the Arab traditions. His day starts, as does the day of every Moslem, with prayers to God, facing Mecca as the sun rises over this new Eastern capital that has sprung up almost overnight on the seven hills that surround the village which, twenty short years ago, was Amman.

By ten o'clock he is at his desk meeting his Prime Minister, being briefed on any new foreign development or internal crisis. At work he listens attentively, sitting with a stillness characteristic of him, concentrated, appreciative. Then he makes his decision, with a realism that has always been one of his chief political assets. For example, while President Nasser was still flirting with Russia in the Near East, Hussein never doubted that Communism was the real enemy of the Arab way of life —the life of free men who retain their independence and dignity. Now the Egyptian leader has come round to the King's way of thinking. "Well," says the King, "they are late starting. Let's hope now they catch us up."

During the years of his early kingship, until 1956, he had to fight for his throne. Security was the most important matter he had to tackle, and he tackled it with zest and courage. The Sharif Nasir advises him on security, but the King himself has ideas on this subject, ideas he puts into practice. He knows that on him depends the survival of Arab kingship in a new tradition, modern Arab kingship which he had hoped to establish for all time with the co-operation of his cousin, King Faisal of

Iraq. Now, however, Hussein alone must carry this burden, in order that his own House may survive.

In this respect he has had to deal with extraordinary moments of crisis. Two days before the Iraq Revolution his aide and confidant, Colonel Rahdi el-Abdullah, was found to be false to the King. The discovery that one so close to his person could have joined his enemies distressed the King greatly. In April 1957 Major-General Ali Abu Nuwar, who had taken the place of General Glubb as Chief of Staff, was found to be plotting against the King. The King saved Nuwar from death by giving him a quick exile—an act of compassion that was not universally approved.

He does not spend half his working day at his desk. More time is taken up by meeting people. His court is always open to the people of Jordan. The last time I visited the King at the Basman Palace the visitors included sheikhs who had come to urge action to save animals in their district threatened by the drought, a British currency expert who was going on leave, an American Senator and his wife who were 'doing' Jordan, a Foreign Office official who had been appointed to an important post abroad, an official of the Phillips Company reporting to the King on progress in the oil-field, and half a dozen other parties who, for some reason, urgent and important to their community, had come to invoke the King's aid.

The *New York Times*, in a penetrating article, summed up the qualifications that are enabling King Hussein to dominate the Jordan, and, to an extent, the Arab scene. During my prolonged stay in Jordan I was able to confirm the correctness of the American diagnosis.

"Hussein has three principal assets; his courage, his birthright as the descendant of the Prophet Mohammed, and British and American support."

To that I would add the unswerving allegiance of the bedouin Arabs, on whom he relies more and more, and from whose ranks the Jordan Army is increasingly recruited. Certainly the King's birth and his courage, which perhaps stems from it, are his greatest assets. The support of the United States and Britain help Jordan to balance her budget, and such help cannot be dispensed with at present. Close alliance with the West is of course by no means an unmixed blessing for an Arab ruler. He is liable to constant attack and misrepresentation on this account. My most abiding impression of Hussein is that he takes the Jordanian view always, looking out at the world from Jordan, not in at Jordan from without—the viewpoint of foreign writers. Thus the King is not so much concerned in his day-to-day contacts with the Power politics of the great East-West struggle—a struggle of economic and political creeds: he is concerned with grappling with the immediate issues that affect his people. Water, prices, currency, taxes, import duties, oil discovery, agricultural reform—all these exercise the King's mind, for they are problems very near to the Jordan people, the people for whom the King unceasingly works.

The King has no vanity of dress. He will wear with composure a suit he has outgrown, or a suit rather too large for him. Kingship, he believes, rests in the soul of a man. If he has faith he will win. If he has weakness and vacillation he will lose. It is the teaching of the Koran, and there is no doubt that perhaps without knowing it Hussein has taken to heart the personal lesson of the history of the Prophet. For in the founder of Islam the world saw a man supremely master of himself and, accordingly, the master of his world. "Discipline," said the Prophet, "is the beginning of greatness."

This young King has discipline. He lives frugally. His relaxations are taken with open eyes. In Amman it could be truly said, the King's eyes are clear—whatever there is to see, he will see it, unafraid.

He spends much time away from the palace. Often he will leave his study by nine, pass down the broad steps, past the picturesque Circassian Guard—a traditional line of servants to his House—and step into one of the waiting cars. Then the cavalcade moves off at speed.

On one of his routine visits to the Zerqa Camp, Army Headquarters, from nine-thirty till five the King greeted his officers and men, shaking hands, talking, until finally he was through. Stepping into his car, he said a few parting words through a microphone. Back to him came the roar of his soldiers, "We are loyal to thee unto death, Hussein!"

It is this kind of experience that has made the King, in his own words, a dedicated servant of the Jordan people. In an age when strong belief and conviction, except in Communist countries, is thought out-moded, when disillusion is the fashion, and every one seeks to see all sides of all problems, the single-mindedness of King Hussein stands out. He has a creed:

He believes in the new State of Jordan.

He believes that Jordan will survive and prosper.

He believes in his own mission as an Arab King.

He believes that the Prophet protects him for a good and useful purpose—"No, sir, I fear no one but God."

It seems almost incredible now that as recently as 1958 the King was reading reports of his impending extinction, in his study in the Basman Palace, written, not by sensation-seeking journalists, but by reporters of repute. I was handed some of these reports in the palace, the significant passages underlined in red ink, and annotated in Arabic. Such reports would have been enough to sap the courage of a man less resolute than Hussein.

In the respected *Washington Post* Ernest K. Lindley was writing:

> Let us take the responsibility of an orderly determination of the future of Jordan. This weak, divided little country cannot expect to endure as an independent nation. Hussein probably will leave when the British do [British troops flew to Jordan for three months at the King's request at the time of the murder of his cousin, King Faisal of Iraq, for which the murderers have not yet been arrested]. But a coup leading to fusion with the United Arab Republic might touch off war.

When the King read this fantastic declaration he must have thought, I can deal with my enemies, but God preserve me from my friends.

But it was not only the American Press that was so ready, even eager, to write off the State of Jordan. Iain Lang, as fine a journalist as Fleet Street can show to-day, was writing in the *Sunday Times* in a vein of gloomy nostalgia, with a hint of doom. Under the title, "Can King Hussein Survive?" he wrote in August 1959, "When the King drives out from his palace his car is escorted by twelve jeeps, each carrying four soldiers armed with Bren-guns. Even when he visited the British Brigade his forty-eight man bodyguard, fingers on triggers, surrounded him while he was inspecting the guard of honour."

If this period of acute tension did in fact exist it soon passed, for later the same year the King was motoring privately in Jordan, in a cavalcade of three cars, while in London very recently he walked alone and unguarded from a meeting back to his hotel.

The *Sunday Times* went on to review the past with a strong hint that history might repeat itself. "He is the last, hardpressed survivor of a once great Arab dynasty. Forty years ago in the Hauran desert I watched the entry of the Sharifian forces into Deraa, led by Hussein's great-uncle, the Emir Faisal. Another Hussein was the powerful King of the Hejaz. Within a year he was exiled in Cyprus. Now Iraq too is lost to the Hashemites. Only Jordan remains. . . ."

Only great courage and tenacity of purpose could have enabled Hussein to carry on at a time when he was being abused in Cairo, hated in Baghdad, and written off as a forlorn hope by the West. Now that has changed, but the change of heart and purpose has not been achieved by wise counsels in the State Department or the sagacity of the British Foreign Office. The change has been brought about by the determination of one young man who believes in his own destiny.

Speculating as to what extent Hussein's upbringing still moulds his character is a fascinating occupation. If he learnt one lesson at Sandhurst it was—never give up. If Harrow taught him anything it was—exercise composure and politeness in adversity. Hussein is a Jordanian first, last, and all the time, but it may not be far-fetched to suggest that he has one characteristic which he shares with the British people : the reluctance, however adverse the circumstances, to accept defeat. And because he will not accept defeat he will win.

At any time we may ask for an audience with the King, and, having secured it, pass up through the wrought-iron gates, past the Circassian Guard, to the white steps that lead to the palace door. On our left is the waiting-room, on our right the King's study, a simple room with a desk and a fine portrait of the great Abdullah.

We may have to wait, for the King often overruns his interviews, but then we will be served Turkish coffee by a turbaned servant with a gold dagger in his belt. We will talk to the King's other guests, and always the talk will be of Jordan and her future.

Soon he is ready for us, dressed to-day as a Marshal of his own Air Force. As he sees us, the dark, serious young face lights up with that smile that the people of Jordan instantly recognize. It is a smile of warmth and even gaiety. I can only recall one other man who had it in the same degree : the Duke of Windsor as a very youthful Prince of Wales—he had a captivating smile.

"Come in! Sit down. Glad to see you again. Welcome!"

So attractive is the personality of King Hussein that it is all too easy for visitors to Jordan to forget the very real dangers with which the King is faced, and which, sooner or later, he will have to dispel.

Talking with persons of varying interests and differing political attitudes in Jordan, I came to the conclusion that the following are the key questions that now face the King:

First, the settlement of the Israeli problem; and with this is bound up the solution of the refugee situation. A state of war between the Arab states and Israel cannot continue indefinitely. No Arab leader has dared to make a move towards peace. If Hussein were able to do so he would at one stroke become the leader of the Arab world. It is well known that Israel seeks a solution, and is ready, by compensation and other means, to go far farther towards a peaceful solution than is publicly admitted.

Secondly, the King has to regulate his relationship with other Arab states. In reopening diplomatic relations with President Nasser of Egypt, the King has taken the first step in this direction.

Thirdly, perhaps the greatest task that faces the King and his Government is to make Jordan financially free of foreign aid, both American and British, and to raise the standard of living, both of the farmer and the town-dweller, in Jordan to a level where Communism no longer makes any appeal.

These are great tasks. The first is deeply connected with world peace as well as peace in the Middle East. But all three problems demand vision.

Hussein is already a King. Can he become a Prophet? Has he in him the stuff of greatness? Or will greatness be thrust upon him?

Those very close to this young man have a great responsibility; to use their influence for progress, however dangerous and difficult the path of progress may appear to be.

3

The King and Glubb Pasha

Note

I believe that no full and true account of the dismissal
of Glubb Pasha and the reasons that lay behind it has
hitherto been published.

In the chapter that follows I have told the whole story
without fear or favour because, in its way, the story reveals
the characteristic growth of Jordanian national feeling and
of the King's determination to make Jordan fully independent. It is too often forgotten that what the new nations of
the Near and Middle East most ardently want is absolute
freedom. The fact that the British or Americans excel in
certain aspects of diplomacy, administration, or technique
does not interest them. They greatly prefer an indifferent
Arab product to an excellent foreign product, in ideas as
in goods, and of course they are right.

I have told the story of General Glubb and the King
early in the book because it is so indicative. By accident
and good fortune accounts of this matter reached me that
were completely authentic, but not obtainable in the
ordinary way. The Levant Department of the British
Foreign Office and the American State Department have
not got these documents that give the Jordanian view of the
dismissal of General Glubb. Now they are not obtainable
in Jordan, either.

For this reason, and because of its intrinsic importance,
I hope that the chapter that follows will shed a new light on

events that, if properly understood, illuminate the entire course of recent events in Jordan.

I have taken the greatest care to check my account with the Arab and English bibliography on the subject. I am now confident that this is the true story.

In the early morning of March 2, 1956, King Hussein surprised the world by dismissing John Bagot Glubb who, as General Glubb, C.M.G., C.B.E., M.C.—known in Jordan as Glubb Pasha—commanded the Arab Legion.

The act caused consternation to the British Government who, apparently, had received no warning of any such intention from their Ambassador in Amman. The speed with which General Glubb was removed from his post, and the lack of ceremony accorded him, gave offence to the British public, to whom General Glubb had become a legend, almost a tradition.

The incident, only one in many swift events that have coloured the history of Jordan, is so revealing that it repays close study. The personalities involved, vivid and characteristic though they are, are dwarfed by the surge of events, by the onward rush of Arab nationalism, which no man, King or President, can afford to ignore.

General Glubb personified, to the Jordanians, a long line of Englishmen who had moved among them as figures of power with influence in high places. For nearly a quarter of a century these men were not resented. They were respected, and received what they had earned—the gratitude of the Arab peoples. Liberation from four hundred years of Turkish domination might not have been achieved by the Emir Faisal without the tenacity and courage of Lawrence, that strange, twisted little Englishman of incomparable genius. The modern Jordan

Army owes a great deal, even to-day, to the influence and inspiration of Peake Pasha, its first commander. And General Glubb, in his years of command, immensely improved the morale, the efficiency, and the conditions of service of the Arab Legion he controlled with a handful of British and a large number of Jordanian officers.

It was not unnatural that the British Government should regard General Glubb and the other officers seconded for service in Jordan as part and parcel of the life of the young nation, and as part of the Anglo-Jordan Treaty and the subsidiary agreements that provided British finance for Jordan's armed forces. But it was short-sighted. It showed that the depth and the direction of the Arab revolution was not fully appreciated in London. To a Jordanian, the facts seemed very different.

Britain had helped to liberate the whole of the Near East from Ottoman rule. To that extent she was welcomed to play a leading rôle in the development of the nations to whom she had given life. The links between Britain and Iraq, Jordan, and Egypt were very strong, as were French ties with the Lebanon and Syria. But every Arab saw in the continuing power of the British and French spheres of influence a real and ever-present danger. Were they to be rid of the Turks merely to receive a new domination directed from London and Paris?

President Nasser was asking this question in Cairo, and giving a certain No as the answer. The influence of Nasser throughout the Near East is often rated far too low. His personal political relations with the other Near Eastern rulers may fluctuate from week to week, almost from day to day, but his influence with the Arab masses is undoubted, and permeates the new nations. His name and his mission are recognized in Baghdad, Damascus, Amman, Beirut; wherever crowds of Arabs forgather. He is essentially a popular hero. He is the man who repelled the British invasion of Egypt. He is the man who, by some high magic, drove the Israeli forces from the Sinai peninsula. This may be a view of events that no one who knows the facts can accept, but it is accepted by millions of Arabs.

But the influence of Nasser does not stop at the large, illiterate crowds who are apt to swarm into the streets of all the Near East cities, seeking mob-rule. If it did, it would not be a decisive factor. The armies control these countries—not the politicians, in the last resort, but the armed forces. President Nasser has made a great impact on the new cadre of Arab army officers in all the new Arab states. To these young professional soldiers, he is the man who would support the dignity, the independence, and the financial and social standing of the Arab armies.

It is necessary to remember that honour, often taking the form of pride, is a decisive Arab characteristic.

The young Jordanian officers have read history. They know that before civilization had reached Britain, France, or Germany, except for the awakening of Christianity, the Arab armies, propelled by the memory of the Prophet, had conquered the Near East, North Africa, Spain, and had marched victoriously into France. The flag of Islam was the flag of the rulers from the Persian Gulf to the Pyrenees. Why, now, should they be subject to any kind of restraint or undue influence—far less orders—from the nationals of the 'colonial' Powers?

All these factors moulded the relationship between the

King and his Chief of Staff, General Nuwar, who replaced General Glubb.

Nuwar was an able officer of the new school. He disliked and distrusted not so much General Glubb—it would be difficult not to like and respect so loyal and good a friend—but all Glubb stood for. And the year 1956 gave Nuwar, and all who thought as he did, a unique opportunity of pressing their views on King Hussein.

For the first time the temper of the people of Jordan had exploded into great mass demonstrations in Amman and Jerusalem. The banners of the protest meetings were all the same. "Release the officers charged with sedition!" "Eisenhower, take your hands off Jordan!" "Get rid of the British Imperialists!"

Now the mobs could only be effectively controlled by stern measures, measures that would have to be taken by the Army, for the Police were not powerful enough to control the crowds. And on more than one occasion it was seen that troops sent to disperse a multitude of demonstrators tended to be overwhelmed by the crowd, and to join them as brothers.

The root cause of this was thought to be the 'British-officer clique' which controlled the Arab Legion. The young King was told, quite rightly, that his troops were loyal to him. It was but a short step, in the counsels of Nuwar, to add that they could no longer be expected, in this political climate, to recognize or accept any further British control of the Army.

Hussein accepted this argument. If we can set aside the special relationship that had grown up between Jordan and Britain, looking only at the situation as it was and as it promised to develop, there can be little doubt that the King was right. General Glubb had to go. He was the outward and visible sign of an era that had passed. The pity of it was that his going could not have been contrived with that dignity and courtesy on which the Jordanians rightly pride themselves.

There were other factors that explain both the reason for his dismissal and the haste of his departure.

Two charges were made against General Glubb by the Left-wing parties in Jordan. Neither were true, but the average Jordanian believed they were, and politics is the art of mastering the dominating influences at work among a people.

The first charge was that during the Arab-Israeli conflict the general was not "faithful" to Jordan, but appeared to regard himself as, in some sense, an umpire, seeing that there was fair play between the Jews and the Arabs. Now, in view of the Treaty relationship between Jordan and Britain and the fact that Britain, in the first place, had taken a great part in the creation of the State of Israel, carved from the British Palestine Mandate, it would not have been at all strange if General Glubb had reflected the views of the British Government, who were hoping—almost praying—that Arab and Jew would live together in peace as they had done in the golden days of the mandate which had brought so much prosperity to Palestine.

In fact, General Glubb never took this extra-Jordanian political approach to his job. Contrary to the allegations made afterwards, throughout the whole of the armed conflict in 1946 and 1947 he procured the best arms he could for the Army under his command, and his orders

to evacuate certain towns, or portions of cities, a part of
Jerusalem, Lod, and Ramla were given to contain his
forces as a mobile striking-power and for no other reason.
Even the more extreme Jordanian politicians now realize
that the charges made against King Farouk—which were
equally baseless, for the King was, and is, an Egyptian
patriot—did not apply at any time to General Glubb.
Yet the allegations had their effect. They were a part and
parcel of the stock arguments of the Jordanian opposition
to Glubb Pasha.

Much more effective, though equally without sub-
stance, were the charges against General Glubb for
'gerrymandering' the Jordan elections.

The official opposition view of this matter was expressed
in this way:

> In all previous [pre-1956] elections Glubb's influence was
> clearly shown. He had not been satisfied with imposing his
> power on the Army. He also imposed it on the Government.
> According to the law, the Army had to vote in its camps.
> No one, not even the Prime Minister, had the power to
> supervise the elections in the camps. Under this system the
> Army would elect those chosen by General Glubb. He used to
> send orders to the camp captains requiring them to procure
> the election of certain candidates. The captains had to report
> the results to Glubb, who would himself inform the Govern-
> ment of the voting. The candidate's destiny was in the hands
> of Glubb. He would rise or fall according to Glubb's wishes.

This picture, so obviously partial and distorted, is not
without its humorous aspect. No doubt that in the well-
drilled ranks and Officers Corps of the Legion ambitious
young commanders were loath to submit a list to the
general which they thought might incur his displeasure.

The result was a remarkable uniformity of voting by the Army. The camps returned what were termed 'Glubb men' with very few exceptions.

And the moral, from a Jordanian standpoint, is drawn in this heartfelt paragraph again quoted from the official opposition view:

> Since the so-called representatives of the people in Parliament were in effect chosen by Glubb, it was felt that those representatives were not working for the good of the Arab people. Glubb would never choose a man who was pro-Arab, if he was anti-British. He wanted to serve the British imperialistic interests in Jordan. During the October 1956 elections in Jordan Glubb was not present to control elections. The opportunity was given to the people to elect freely whom they wanted. The people, seeing the secret ballot, and the open counting of votes, felt that the elections were free and honest.

The King watched the result of this election with the closest interest. Here, he thought, was a clear indication of the trend of popular opinion among the Jordanian people. There were 144 candidates for the forty seats. Liberals and Independents described as being anti-Israeli, anti-Imperialist, and anti all Western influence swept the board. The extremist parties met with little success. It was a huge majority for the anti-Western moderates, mainly Independents. I shall give detailed results of this election, and present Jordanian views on the various parties, in Chapter 10.

King Hussein, viewing the result, could not but be impressed. The explosion of political freedom in Jordan was not throwing up extremists, but the verdict against Western domination in Jordan itself seemed to be decisive.

The King took this to mean that he was free to maintain his good relations with the West, with Britain in particular, provided that such relations were on a basis of absolute equality. But there was one great factor that made this almost impossible—the permanent deficit in the Jordanian budget. The fact that Jordan, in her present boundaries, until oil or other extraordinary wealth is discovered, can never hope in the immediate future to balance her income and expenditure, makes her relations with the West a creditor-debtor relationship, and that relationship, with all the good will in the world, is never a relationship of absolute equality.

When the King accepted Nuwar's recommendation that Glubb should go the question arose as to how this should be done. The King was in Amman, working in the Basman Palace. General Glubb was at Zerqa, at Army Headquarters. In a physical sense he virtually controlled the country. Sixty thousand armed men, with tanks and planes, were under his command. The Jordanian officers who had urged the King to dismiss him still feared and respected him. The habit of obedience was strong in the Jordan armed forces. Moreover, Glubb Pasha spoke Arabic. He was the last of the great Englishmen who have had firm friendships with the bedouin Arabs. Some of the sheikhs were still powerful. The Sheikh Mithcal Faiz, for example, controlled over thirty thousand armed men. And another nightmare haunted the anti-Glubb faction. How would Britain react to an announcement that General Glubb had been dismissed? Might she not fly troops into Jordan 'to restore order' in pursuance of Treaty rights?

King Hussein would greatly have preferred to part

with his old and faithful servant with decorum and decency. It would have been Jordan saying good-bye to an era that was over. The general, after a ceremonial march past of the troops to whom he had given the best years of his life, would have received, at the King's hands, the highest Jordanian decoration. He would have flown out of Jordan accompanied, on the first part of his journey to London, by an escort of the Royal Jordanian Air Force.

Rightly or wrongly, however, this procedure was deemed too risky. It was decided that the knot must be cut with lightning quickness—that Glubb should be on his way out of Jordan when the news reached the world.

And so it was done. The Arab world was elated. President Nasser, in conference with the British Foreign Secretary, told him the news with relish. It was hailed as a supreme setback to the British in the Near East. King Hussein received a fervid welcome the first time he reappeared before a multitude of his own people. But to the officers who had engineered the coup, it was the first step in their ultimate designs. Nuwar took the place of Glubb after an interval of a few months. As soon as he was in power he started to plot to bring Jordan in line with the policy and interests of Egypt. The idea of a United Arab Republic was to mean, in actual terms, initially, a combined nation, completely encircling Israel, and stretching from Cairo to the Turkish border.

The King heard of these designs in time, and Nuwar was arrested—and exiled.

As a personal footnote to this chapter on the King and General Glubb I can add the following story:

During the visit of King Hussein to London, the King

made a great impact and impression on the Cabinet and the Press. Although his was not a State visit, yet he was visiting Britain as King of Jordan for the first time since Glubb's dismissal.

The climax of the visit, apart from the King's meetings with the Queen and her family, was a great reception held at the Jordan Embassy, in London.

I entered the receiving-room immediately after General Glubb. The young King was standing by himself, receiving, one after the other, the highest representatives of the British Government in all its fields, the armed services as well as the Foreign Office, the Opposition, and the Cabinet. He bore his habitual look of absolute serenity—what one man who knows him has described as 'desert dignity.' He was cordial, polite, regal. But when he saw his old general enter his face lit up with the smile that those who know him recognize as being the smile of friendship. For the first time he took a step forward and greeted the general. He smiled as if greeting an old friend; or perhaps he recalled that his grandfather King Abdullah, had said of Glubb, "He is one of us."

4

The King as Political Leader

It is almost impossible for those who have the good fortune to live under settled constitutional monarchy to realize the difficulties that have assailed King Hussein ever since that day of May 2, 1953, when, as a young man of eighteen, he took the oath as King to support and uphold the Kingdom of Jordan.

In Europe the constitutional monarchies—Britain, Holland, Belgium, Denmark, Sweden, and Norway—represent the highest standard of living and the greatest degree of political democracy so far obtained. They compare very favourably with countries that have adopted other systems, such as France, Spain, the United States, and the Soviet Union. In Jordan, on the other hand, the King's task was a direct and personal challenge. Enemies of Jordan were determined to destroy the young State, and to do this quickly.

Now, the enemies of Jordan were two. First came International Communism, behind which stood the immense resources of the Soviet Union—and to the ranks of Communism President Nasser was at this time an ardent and vociferous recruit. The second enemy was Israel. It was not expected that if Jordan stood firm Israel would attack Jordan. The Jordanian Army was respected and feared abroad. But if there were signs of collapse in Jordan, if the young State was

48

King Hussein with the author in the study of the Basman Palace, Amman

By courtesy of Studio Angelo

48

King Hussein with the wives of his officials

Court martial of the officers who took part in the attempted coup

By courtesy of Studio Angelo

Dignitaries express their loyalty in the Basman Palace after the 1956 troubles

not able to stand because of constant political agitation or economic bankruptcy, then, the King felt sure, the Israeli forces would advance, and take the left bank—and who could say whether they would stop there?

The King has never been in any doubt about International Communism. "It is an evil thing—the Powers of Darkness. It would destroy the Faith by which we live." Here we have no 'sweet reasonableness,' as affected by liberal Western politicians. The King believes that the system of government that has been set up in the Soviet Union and in her satellite countries is an evil police dictatorship in which no man can call his soul his own. The citizen cannot say what he likes, cannot pray as he likes, cannot even associate with others in public meeting, or form a party. No one has been told the number of political prisoners in Soviet gaols, and the conditions that obtain there.

If and when the Russian dictatorship is overthrown, and a constitutional monarchy restored to that country, the tale of persecution and torture from 1917 onward will be the epic horror story of all time.

On the Israeli question the King reflects the view of the average Jordanian. There can be no peace until the refugee problem is settled.

It is not possible in a short biography to detail the entire political activity of His Majesty from the day he became King until now, but at least it is possible to indicate the pattern and to take a critical, and not untypical, ten days when the King was most hard-pressed.

The pattern from the start has been danger from

disloyalty in the highest ranks of the Army, and danger from the riots in the streets.

The rank and file of the Jordan Army have shown again and again that they support their King, if necessary with their lives. Many Palestinian Arab officers, and all the bedouin officers, have been equally loyal, but there was a small group of officers who had sold themselves either to Egypt or to the Soviet Union, and to the Communists. These men held high positions, and constituted the most immediate danger to the King. At the same time that the King was facing this dual political threat his country had constant money trouble. The financial deficit was acute, but this is a matter to be dealt with elsewhere.

As an example of the tumult of events, let us take April 1957. It is the month of Ramadhan, the Moslem Fast. During this time the extraordinary conditions of life imposed by the Moslem Faith, and the discipline required, adds to the heated and explosive atmosphere which is common in the Near East.

As Prime Minister the King had Mr Suliman Nabulsi, who was pro-Egyptian and anti-Western to a remarkable degree. As his Chief of Staff the King had General Nuwar, who was secretly plotting against the palace. The situation was dynamite.

Nabulsi controlled the street mobs, who could be whipped into lynching mood at a moment's notice. General Nuwar was an able and influential commander. On April 10 Hussein dismissed Nabulsi. He directed Said el-Mufti, the President of the Senate, to form a Government. Then Nuwar made his mistake. He sent for Said el-Mufti, and warned him that he should withdraw, and allow a Leftist leader to take his place.

The King, who hears everything, heard of this very quickly.

Article 35 of the Jordanian Constitution is clear and short: "The King appoints the Prime Minister, dismisses him, or accepts his resignation from Office."

As rioting broke out in Nablus, Jerusalem, and Amman, the King was informed by his loyal bedouin officers that units under the command of General Nuwar were on the move. Their objective was the Basman Palace. The commander of the Armoured Corps was said to be ready to support him. Fresh rioting broke out in the provinces, and there were clashes between loyal and traitorous sections of the Army at Zerqa and at Ajlun.

Jordan was going up in smoke. The pattern of revolt that was to consume Iraq the following year, and introduce overt Communism into Baghdad, was about to burst into flames in the streets of Amman. Within hours a military dictatorship, favourable to the Soviet Union and those who supported it would be established.

The King could easily have left his post at this time. He could have flown to Beirut, Cyprus, or even Malta. At the risk of his life, he called for his car, and drove straight to the Zerqa Army Headquarters. There, in a passionate appeal, by the force of his personality and his kingly courage, he quelled the revolt.

Three days later General Nuwar was summoned to the palace and arrested. In an act of compassion without precedent in the fierce kaleidoscope of Eastern politics, Nuwar was not put to death. He was exiled to Syria. There, later, he was joined by his deputy, General Ali

Hayyari. Both these officers went to work for the Egyptian Government, in its new form of the United Arab Republic.

Major-General Haaza Majali, an officer of bedouin extraction, was appointed to the supremely important post of Chief of Staff.

Nothing can exceed the spite and frustration which the King's victory provoked. The Egyptian Press broke into a stream of unrestrained, vitriolic abuse against the young King, against his mother, and against the new Prime Minister, Dr Hussein Khalidi. The Soviet Press supported with inspired comments, stating that the King, with Western military attachés in Amman, was plotting a coup to place Jordan directly under Western domination.

Any one who has seen at first hand the real relationship between the palace and the American and British Ambassadors in Jordan knows how fantastic this story is, but it was believed by millions in the United Arab Republic, who take their views from a rigidly controlled Press.

On April 24 a message was received from Mr Dulles assuring the King that the United States was concerned with the independence of Jordan and determined to maintain it. This was far short of a declaration that Hussein had the unqualified support of the United States, but it was encouraging. On that day the street mobs called out in Amman met with stern resistance.

April 24 was a busy day for King Hussein. He did the following things:

He warned Egypt and Syria—the United Arab Republic—that Iraq was ready and willing to come to the aid of Jordan if Jordan was invaded from abroad.

He made a public announcement that International Communism, not the free will of the Jordan people, was at the root of all the trouble.

He closed the Jordan-Syria frontier, to seal off the infiltration of Communists from the North.

He was also in hourly contact with his Army and Police chiefs as to the general situation. In the evening of the same day the Prime Minister, Khalidi, resigned. Martial law was declared, and a curfew was clamped on the large towns.

This show of force and determination had quick repercussions abroad. King Saud telegraphed congratulating King Hussein on his control of a dangerous situation. Egypt suddenly denied that her Government desired the disintegration of Jordan. Friends appeared on the horizon.

On April 27 King Hussein was given a special credit of ten million dollars by the United States Government, a timely and solid sign of support. The King's success was making itself felt in Washington.

On May 1, the first day of 'Id el-Fitr, the Moslem festival that marks the end of Ramadhan, and the breaking of the Fast, the tension in Jordan began to relax. The curfew was lifted in Amman. The King received a deputation of three hundred sheikhs, who came and staged a fervid demonstration of loyalty in Amman, cheering the young King for minutes on end. The King visited the Zerqa Army Headquarters, where he was surrounded by thousands of Jordanian soldiers and their officers, and given a welcome the like of which can seldom have been witnessed in modern history.

The King made a public statement. The Soviet Union, he said, was determined to procure the assassinations of:

King Faisal of Iraq
King Saud of Saudi Arabia
the King of Jordan
King Idris of Libya

The first king on the list met his death, murdered by the Forces of a quasi-Communist revolutionary regime.

The statement ended by saying that General Nuwar had received a huge sum of money through the Egyptian Embassy, Amman, for the purpose of procuring the death of the King. Documents to prove this were said to be in the hands of the authorities.

By this time the King and the people of Jordan had suffered considerable strain. Even so, their powers of resistance were to be tried still farther. In November, when the trial of the officers accused of having plotted against the King during the previous April was held, the situation was rendered doubly acute by Radio Cairo's efforts to foment dissension in Jordan, and by the virulence of their personal attacks on King Hussein. Again there were enacted scenes of wild turbulence in Amman.

Moreover, the Communists, having failed to incite the Jordan Army against the King, now endeavoured to persuade the refugees in Jordan to assassinate him. The refugees were not to be won over, however, for the reason that the King—with a gesture of unparalleled generosity —had granted them Jordanian citizenship. They showed no inclination to assassinate their benefactor.

With the exception of Saudi Arabia, the Arab states then made an effort to strangle Jordan economically by retracting their promise of financial aid; but this *volte-face* did not have the hoped-for effect, as aid to Jordan was renewed by the United States and Great Britain.

On New Year's Eve 1957 Samir Rifai, the new Foreign Minister, later to become Prime Minister, was able to say, "The immediate danger is over. Order is restored. Egyptian and Syrian threats, hitherto a serious menace, are no longer a danger to us."

The people started to turn in their thousands to the King's way of thinking. Wherever he went the same crowds who, months before, had cried out against his rule, now flocked to his banner. It was the King's courage, and nothing else, that had won them over.

We are apt to regard the new stability in Jordan as being the result of the wisdom and support of the United States and the United Kingdom, and certainly they played their part. So, too, did the arrival by air of a small, but well equipped, British force at the time of the Iraq Revolution. But the basic and deciding factor has been the attitude of the Jordanian people to their King. One Palestinian told me, "In certain parts of the country, at one time over 80 per cent. of the people opposed Hussein and his House. Now you might say that the King has won the support of the majority everywhere. Moreover, a new spirit has arisen; a feeling that we are no longer Palestinians or bedouin, but Jordanians. This new national spirit is vitally important. It is what the King has been trying to achieve. He has achieved it."

Those who think that the King could have accomplished this by the early introduction of a complete democracy when he assumed the throne are mistaken. For four centuries these people had been subject to political discipline, with considerable personal freedom. The Sultan only struck if he saw a rebel. Then he struck with death. And so it was that Hussein had first to win his spurs, to impose himself on the image of the Jordan people. This he did, and now they look to him to lead them in more liberal ways.

With the New Year of 1958 came new hope too. The King's wise and kindly acts were remembered. His gifts of land to small farmers; his decision to get rid of the last traces of foreign control over the Jordanian Army by the dismissal of Glubb Pasha, who was his friend; the control the King himself exercised over his own entourage who, from time to time, urged more stringent, and even savage, penalties for those who had rebelled—all these things were, for the first time, recalled by the Jordanian people. Where-ever one went one heard the King well spoken of. The least that was said of him by his former enemies was, "He has great courage. Nothing else could have saved Jordan."

There is one aspect of Jordan's foreign relations I must again refer to, for it affected the King's position very gravely, and that is the tendency at this time, and at the time of the Iraq Revolution in 1958, of the American and British Governments and Press to 'write off' the King and Jordan as too hopeless a cause to support. This attitude was not finally overcome until the King's visits to Washington and London in 1959, when the British and American Governments entered into an unwritten agreement which I shall discuss in later chapters.

I have cuttings of over twenty articles in the Washing-ton, London, and New York Press which strike this note of doom for King Hussein in his struggle against Eastern Communism. These trends in the Western Press gave great hope and encouragement to our enemies wherever they were read—and they were read, and carefully filed, in every anti-Western capital.

But this attitude did not stop with the Press. Western diplomats in Amman were apt to reflect the general trend. I openly discussed with senior diplomats in Amman, what Western relations might be with a new regime. Jordanians had the impression that visiting British politicians were calculating the odds. "In success we are your friends, in defeat we should have to look elsewhere." No doubt that is practical politics, but the adoption of this attitude has sustained the conviction that many Eastern races hold that the British are a crafty, clever race, friends only to those who can serve their purposes.

The King, to his credit, never wavered. "We must take the situation as we find it. No one will save Jordan but the efforts of the Jordanian people." And to the King, at long last, the Jordan people rally more and more.

I have tried to paint a picture of the young Hussein in action. There has never been any doubt about one matter in Jordan, and that is—where the King stands. He stands against Communism in any shape or form. He stands against Western domination of Eastern nations, including Jordan. He fights to keep alive the Moslem Faith unfettered by foreign influences. And he looks forward to the day when a resurgent Arab nationalism will sweep Communism out of the Near East so that the new states can grow up without fear or persecution, without danger from without or within. London and Washington recognize this now.

We could be prouder if they too had had no reservations in the difficult, dangerous days I have just described.

5
The King's Policies

In order to understand the reactions of King Hussein to any question, external or internal, that affects his Kingdom, it is necessary to know something of Jordanian society and Moslem philosophy, for from this background and Faith spring the motivations of the King's policies.

Jordanian society is a very modern creation. In its present form it only dates back twelve years. It was a part, and not a very large part, of Arab society as a whole. The word Arab indicates a nomad, and the King's people were nomads. They had the culture, pride, and customs of nomads as opposed to the customs and outlook of farmers and labourers.

The King himself comes from one of the greatest of the princely Arab houses, and it is only very recently that these rulers have fitted into the pattern of the city, and accepted their quota of Western ways.

The religion of Jordan is Islam, and Islam again sets values not common in the West; manhood, nobility, pride, honour, all play a much more important part in Moslem life than they do in Bonn or in Paris. The race for money as such has not corrupted Jordan to the extent that it has corrupted more westernized Eastern states such as Egypt.

Allah is all protecting, merciful, the supreme arbiter

of good and evil. The dignity of man is supremely important, and this leads to intense individual and national pride. The Arabs have never—yet—been able to agree among themselves, but they are agreed on this —that they do not want to be ruled or bullied by foreigners. There is a tremendous feeling in all the Arab states, including Jordan, that all Arab nations have a common heritage, and a common way of life. There is no doubt that if threatened from outside, the Arab states, whatever their differences, would combine for mutual protection. Arabs consider themselves superior to non-Arabs, and the creation of the new independent Arab states has merely given this feeling an outlet. This is the background from which Jordanian policies are built. It is interesting to note what this means in concrete relations with foreign powers.

King Hussein, in every decision he takes, puts his own country and people first. Whether his decisions will be well received in Washington or London is a very secondary consideration. He hopes that his friends will always be friends—loyalty is a great Arab virtue, treachery the ultimate abomination—but he does what appears to him to be right.

In his relations with Britain this attitude has some strange results. The King dismissed Glubb Pasha because, at the time, he was persuaded that this was in the best interest of Jordan. Immediately the British reaction was that the King had become 'anti-British.' He had not. Though the British Government retaliated by recalling other officers, and by becoming 'sticky' in financial matters, the King pursued his overall policy of friend-ship with Britain, now completely restored.

Jordanian relationship with the United States is more complicated. All Arab nations believe that the Americans, while deriding colonialism, are desperately anxious to take over such parts of the British Empire that on attaining complete self-government may be available for exploitation. They say that British and American diplomats are not 'faithful' to each other, but will turn and rend the other ally as soon as he is out of the room. There is undoubtedly some truth in this, but there is also much healthy rivalry. I have watched, for instance, the struggle of American business to get a foothold in the market of Thailand over two decades; but it is strongly held by Chinese and British business interests more efficient than their American rivals. The story has been repeated elsewhere.

The Jordanians say that every petty American official, and all the politicians and military men, have the same objective—to promote purely American interests. To this extent the Jordanian reaction to American generosity and aid is very cautious. American diplomats who know Jordan deplored this trend. "We have told the State Department again and again that aid wrapped up in the Stars and Stripes is suspect. But do they listen? No, sir! It all comes here packaged as before."

Quite recently many millions have been spent by the United States in making the modern Jerusalem-Amman highway for the Jordanians. I motored gratefully over this magnificent highway, but Jordanian reaction is, "The old road was quite adequate [the road built by the British under the mandate]. This new road, though it looks very nice, is shoddy and won't last, and in any case we do not need a road. If there are millions to be spent, then let us have artesian wells and new irrigation schemes."

This kind of reaction is regarded as carping by visiting Senators and other uninitiated visitors, and certainly we are confronted here with two worlds who do not speak the same language.

The King's own attitude towards his Arab neighbours is extremely revealing. There is no doubt that, in Jordan, Quassem and Nasser are looked upon as upstarts, but for President Nasser there is support in every Arab country because he appears to the people as the young leader who was the first really to stand up to Britain and 'call her bluff.' The King's attitude towards Iraq is naturally one of very marked revulsion, but his relationships with Saudi Arabia, Libya, and the Lebanon are very cordial. He is constantly saying, with complete conviction, that the only real hope for the Middle and Near East is to follow the well-defined trail that Jordan has tried to blaze—independence of the West and the East in policy at home and abroad, coupled with an absolute determination to defeat Communism whenever it appears.

At first sight there might seem to be a certain arrogance in this attitude, but in fact there is not. The King knows —none better—how prone to be led are the Arab multitudes. He knows that before his great tussle with the Communists and quasi-Communists, in 1956, the city crowds were howling against his policies, but when he won, when his policies were vindicated, the same crowds roared for the King.

The King seems to reflect the traditional Arab attitude of having no special regard for France, but a certain feeling for Germany. Eight cadets for military training

61

were received when I was in Jordan, from the rebel Government of Algiers. In spite of the intricacies of the Near Eastern situation, Arab hands do stretch across the sea and the desert to be clasped in friendship; and the bond of a common language, a common law, a common faith, and a common race is never entirely forgotten.

When Western politicians fail to understand King Hussein and his Prime Ministers it is because the Western statesmen are looking in at Jordan from outside, and, moreover, they are constantly attempting to classify, in Western terms, what they see. The neat set of labels, 'pro-American,' 'pro-British,' 'anti-Russian,' 'democratic,' 'autocratic,' and so on, are slapped on the leading aspects of Jordanian policy regardless of the fact that they are meaningless to the people of Jordan.

The King's view is a view looking out from Amman, over the seas to Britain and the United States, to the United Arab Republic, to Turkey and Iraq, to 'Jewish-occupied territory,' to Egypt. The two views reflect entirely different pictures. They are a world and a philosophy apart.

What impact has King Hussein made on the outside world? His courage, personal and moral, and his attitude, "I fear no one but God," came as a surprise and an example to the more wily, sophisticated politicians of the West. There is no doubt that it has paid great dividends. Four years ago Jordan was regarded as a British protégé-state. To-day her independence and integrity are in fact underwritten by the United States and Britain. This means, in plain language, that the West would go to war for Jordan. King Hussein, and no one else, has accomplished this for his country. The news first came out in the London *Daily Mail* as a result of an interview granted to its foreign correspondent, Geoffrey Wakeford, and myself, at Claridges Hotel, by Mr Samir Rifai—at that time King Hussein's Prime Minister.

The interview was an exclusive one. Next day Mr Rifai left Britain before any other newspaper could contact him. But the King, who arrived in London the following week, was questioned about the report. "There is no new Treaty," said the King. There is no new Treaty, but there is a very concrete undertaking by both great Powers to Jordan—and this is the King's handiwork.

To sum up the foreign policies of King Hussein: they are—to promote the interests of the Jordan people first, last, and all the time; to receive financial aid, without political strings, until such time as the Jordanian economy will balance the budget; to oppose Communism in all its guises; to defend and protect the Holy Land and the frontiers of Jordan; and, to champion the Jordan and Arab case against Israel. This does not mean that the King does not seek peace. He does more than that. Almost alone of Eastern leaders, Arab or Jew, by the moderation and modesty of his public utterances, he creates an atmosphere in which peace might prosper.

To the average Jordanian, needless to say, these foreign policies are distant matters. What matters to him is markets for his produce, water for his animals and crops; and on these domestic questions the King has pursued a planned course from the day he took over in Jordan, in 1953.

The King brings a fresh, dynamic approach to the

chronic problem presented by the deficit of the Jordanian Budget. "We must, at all costs, develop our resources," he is quoted as saying. "In the long run no one can help the Jordan people as they can help themselves."

Every new project engages the King's interest, though he and his Ministers never lose sight of, nor cease to pursue, one of their chief aims, which is the development of a plan for a large increase in irrigation. This is of vital importance, as irrigated land can produce four times the food yield of land watered only by rain in Jordan, where the rainfall is not only fitful but meagre. Jordan's dispute with Israel, and the failure to reach any agreement concerning the division of the Jordan waters, constitutes a serious obstacle to the advance of irrigation. Even so, by putting minor local schemes into operation, and by the annual erection of new wells, much is achieved, though not on the grand scale which such a situation demands.

The King's interest in oil is intense. The Iraq Petroleum Company formerly had large concessions in Transjordan, but the company was never over keen on exploiting possible Jordan oil. It may well be that the prospecting work of the Phillips Company will meet with greater success. If they do the financial picture for Jordan will change overnight. The sum required by Jordan for progress with solvency is not so great—perhaps fifteen million pounds a year, or less. This might easily be realized out of oil revenues.

Meanwhile, and in addition to taking a close personal interest in other mineral resources, such as immense quantities of potash which come in various forms from the Dead Sea area, the King keeps a close watch over the

The magnificence of the Desert Patrol

By courtesy of Studio Angelo

Arab Legion cavalry during show jumping

King Hussein in conference with bedouin sheikhs

By courtesy of Studio Angelo

The King with the bedouin

state of Jordan's agriculture—the raising of stock (camels, sheep, and goats) and the cultivation of tobacco—and over her industries: milling, cement, beverages, bricks and tiles, electricity. All constantly come under the King's eye as he works at his desk in the Basman Palace.

The King's political policies are inextricably interwoven with the economic and industrial development of his country. The sturdy Arab independence which he represents can only really be achieved when economic independence is achieved—and it looks as if economic independence cannot be achieved without considerable foreign long- and short-term aid.

Soon after he ascended the throne, Hussein made a characteristic gesture to the small farmers around the little village of Madaba. He gave away 10,000 dunums of land to those who possessed the necessary skill to develop it. It was these same small farmers who, when the 1956 crisis reached its height, rode into Amman and demonstrated in favour of the King—a display of gratitude and loyalty which incensed the Communists, who straightway planted a cell in Madaba, hitherto as feudal and conservative a little community as one is ever likely to come across in a year of travel. Communism, however, is anything but a remote danger to Hussein. Indeed, it lies all about him, and he believes that at present, in Jordan, the choice rests between King and Communism —and Hussein believes passionately in kingship. To the Jordanians themselves, Communism represents materialism as opposed to the Faith of Islam, and the Soviet leaders are quick to make use of this. "Through the priests, the West holds out to you a promise of bliss in the world to come," they say, "but we are concerned to give you a decent standard of living here on earth." Hussein, on the other hand, seeks to bring about material progress without submitting to an alien material philosophy, and he needs to speed his efforts in this direction.

The British and American publics should be told the whole truth about Jordan. They should know that by unpublished but solemn undertakings the Governments of the United States and Britain have acknowledged the existing frontiers of Jordan. Thus if Jordan were attacked the United States and Britain would be her allies.[1] In this novel and serious situation the character and policies of King Hussein assume an interest and importance that they would not otherwise have. Hussein is a key leader in the development of progress and of peace throughout the Moslem world that stretches from Morocco to Zanzibar, from Turkey, in Europe, to Pakistan—three hundred million people who, undoubtedly, one day will join in closer political federation. The importance of Hussein is not to be calculated by Jordan alone. His influence, even his advice, may, as the years go by, stretch far beyond the confines of his present Kingdom.

[1] Apart from the interview with Mr Samir Rifai, then Prime Minister of Jordan, published in a London newspaper, there has been no mention of the great and immediate responsibilities entered into by the Western Allies in any British or American publication. No statement of the real facts has been made either to the House of Commons or to Congress; a curious omission.

6

The King and the Bedouin

King Hussein has a very special relationship with the sheikhs of the great bedouin tribes, still nomadic, who control large areas of desert land across the border into Syria, Iraq, and Saudi Arabia. The bedouin have never recognized the new political divisions of the Arab states by frontiers. The black tents pass over the political barriers swiftly and silently. In this respect only the bedouin are ahead of their times. They have made of the Arab Union a living thing, for to them the Arab lands are one.

Thirty years ago the sheikhs who ruled through their minor sheikhs exercised great power in Jordan, and although, with the formation of the new Kingdom after the war, all deferred to the King, Abdullah, they were, to a great extent, independent. Their link with the Crown was one of loyalty. It still is.

The development of Jordanian communications, and the formation of an efficient central Police Force, aided by a Desert Patrol, has tended to decrease the power of the sheikhs, but, of very recent years, King Hussein has been well content that the Arab Law, Arab customs, and Arab ways should be administered by the sheikhs to their own people, for they now have a new rôle to play in developing the Kingdom of Jordan.

The Palestinian Arabs tend to support the ideologies

of President Nasser of Egypt. The bedouin Jordanian Arabs remain firm in their loyalty to the King, and claim that Jordan itself is a much truer reflection of Arab nationalism than the very mixed Egyptian population; so that the situation has arisen when the King looks more and more to his bedouin to maintain his throne until the day—perhaps not far distant—when Jordan will be recognized as the natural leader of the Arab states, as an anti-Communist nation determined to preserve the Arab way of life.

In the early months of 1959 some remarkable statements by President Nasser showed that he was coming round to the Jordanian point of view, rapidly. When I mentioned this to the King he smiled, and said, "Yes, that is so, but they say one thing to-day, another to-morrow. Let them make up their minds where true Arab interest lies. Then, by all means, join us in our fight."

Hussein recruits the modern Jordan Army from the bedouin Arabs in so far as they have the men available, but the amount of suitable officer material is still not large enough. Palestinians have to be employed in some of the highest posts; and there are many good, loyal, able Palestinian Jordanians. But the bedouin, when he has given his loyalty, is absolute. It is sometimes better to have a less able officer, whose heart is with the King, than a Palestinian with one eye on political movements in the Arab states.

The warmest and most invigorating experience that King Hussein has had since he ascended the throne has been the spontaneous movement of the sheikhs to protect his person whenever danger threatened. After United Arab Republic planes had tried to force the King to land at Damascus—the plot was to engineer an 'abdication,' with the King a virtual prisoner—and the King had landed at Amman airport, safe and sound, the sheikhs rode into the city and up to the palace to show their love and loyalty. The scene is without parallel to-day in any country except Saudi Arabia. Down from the mountains, up from the Madaba plains, from dawn they arrived, riding their Arab horses, driving their large convertible cars, the sheikhs, their sons, their retinues, surging through the narrow dusty streets of Amman up to the Basman Palace to greet the young man who is their acknowledged King.

On my last visit to the King five of the great sheikhs were meeting him immediately before my audience. I talked with them when they came out of his study, and asked an English-speaking sheikh from the North how the King had received them. He said, "As he always does, with Arab courtesy. He knows us all by name, and the names of our fathers—and their fathers. For most of us have ridden with the King's forebears in the old days. We never forget this. We are Arabs. The King is an Arab Prince. He is our man. If danger threatens we will defend him to death. He does not have to ask our help. We shall be there." No one could doubt the sincerity of the speaker.

Hussein is very real, his personality very precious, to these Arab sheikhs. For no one has ever really conquered the bedouin Arabs. The Turks had quasi-treaty relations with them. They did not attempt to control them. The British and the French merely carried on the policy of the Ottoman Empire. Now independence has come. Their Prince is a King. The sheikhs are the supporters of the establishment—of the Kingdom. In a reflected Majesty they feel the importance of their new position as the true guardians of the new, free Arabia.

The sheikhs have not yet adopted the debased moral values in currency to-day. Honour, to them, is more important than money, hospitality more important than business. Hussein reflects these attitudes in his person, and in his ways.

I have seen sheikhs buying goods in the shops of Amman, where one always bargains with the proprietor. The sheikhs never bargain. Either they buy, or they do not buy. To talk of money with a shopkeeper seems to them a most undignified proceeding.

In hospitality they are magnificent. When I visited the venerable Sheikh Mithcal Faiz, who was then eighty-four, he had fever, but the old gentleman insisted on getting out of his bed to greet me. The sheikhs believe in the dignity of man, a living dignity of bearing, mien, and manner. Hussein has all these qualities, and in him the sheikhs see their natural, as well as their legal, leader.

I should not have fully appreciated the very special bond that binds the bedouin to the King unless I had visited the sheikhs in their own tents. Through the courtesy of His Excellency Akef Faiz, the King's Minister of Agriculture, I visited his father, the greatest Jordanian Sheikh, at Madaba.

Amman seems large enough when one is in it—a city on seven hills, dominated by the palace, the mosques, the market, the shops, and the hotels; but one is very quickly out of it. Within ten minutes one is in the country of Jordan. The great, bare, bold line of the hills reminds one of the Sussex Downs, but on a wilder and grander scale. By car and by camel, my wife and I travelled to the black tents, bearing in mind the King's words, "See for yourself. You are free to go anywhere. Form your own impressions of our Kingdom. Tell me what you think."

It was noon by the time we reached Madaba and the Sheikh's stronghold. We sat on sheepskin rugs, talking to the Sheikh and his sons and his men, who had come to support him. I asked the Sheikh about the King. Had he come to visit him lately?

"Indeed, yes. His Majesty was here last year. I have the photographs. There you see the black tents of our people. There are the Royal cars drawn up outside. In this one the King is sitting in my tent. My sheikhs are all around him. He is very close to us."

When the Sheikh said this I realized that here was a bond that no political storm would break. It was so simple, so straightforward, so unpolitical. Treachery, to a sheikh, is the crime of a city-dweller. Loyalty is the virtue of sheikhs.

The Sheikh asked me what I thought about the murder of the King's cousin, Faisal, and his family, in Baghdad. I said that I had read the accounts with horror.

"I too," said the Sheikh. "Whatever they may have thought of Nuri Said, they had nothing against the King. He was a gentle Prince." The Sheikh smiled. "Not strong and resourceful like our King, but kind and wise. Do you know what they did? The King was defended by his loyal guards against the Army. After nearly an hour a dozen men had been killed. Still the King could have escaped. He refused to leave his family and the women. He ordered a cease-fire. That was the last order of their

King, and both sides obeyed it immediately." The Sheikh paused, then continued. "'Come out,' they said. 'You will come to no harm.' The young King led his family out of the palace. The Princesses were each carrying the Koran and praying. The King, the gentle one, walked without fear, his head high, still their King.

"The troops butchered them then and there, with Sten-gun fire, going round to bash in their skulls with the butts of their guns. They found two baby Princesses alive, running screaming from the palace. They turned the Sten-guns on them. Their little bodies were ripped to pieces. That is what happened in Baghdad. Now you know what can happen when Communism comes to the Arabs."

"Communism? But our papers say that the new Iraq Government is not Communist."

"My friend, do not deceive yourself. The Arabs are not like you British—middle-of-the-road walkers. We are either for or against. Either we are Loyalist, or we are Communist. Even in Egypt the real danger is Communism unless the throne is restored."

Talking to these sheikhs in their tents, in Jordan, the Western world seemed very far away. It might be only six hours by Comet or by Caravelle to Paris, but here we were in a different world—the world of Arab values, Arab customs.

These men brought home a point that I was apt to lose sight of—the terrible wound inflicted on Jordan and on the Hashemite House by the murderous Iraq Revolution.

King Hussein and King Faisal had made a success of the Arab Union that merged the states of Jordan and

Iraq. The twin kingdoms had abolished their frontiers, abolished their customs-posts, unified their foreign policy. They were in the process of a far more important merger of their armed forces and Parliaments.

What jealousies did these moves arouse in the hostile, anti-monarchist states? Clearly too much success and achievement by the young kings gave great offence. Here were two young men who endeavoured to bring about Arab unity while others talked. Consequently the revolution in Iraq was directed almost as much against Hussein as against Faisal. The visiting Jordan statesmen[1] were torn to pieces in the streets of Baghdad. It was a bloody, savage, unintelligent protest against progress under the kings.

"Whom can I trust?" King Hussein asked the British and American Ambassadors, who hurried to console him. But soon his courage revived. He decided not to march into Iraq and seize the murderers—which is what should have been done, and, perhaps, if it had not been for Western restraint, would have been done. Instead he sealed off his frontiers, asked for British troops to visit his country for a short period while the crisis was at its height.

To the eternal credit of the British Government, that call for aid—the only one Hussein has ever made—was promptly complied with. The 'Red Devils' flew into Amman, the Americans into Beirut. The tide of Communism ebbed.

The young King himself is far in advance of the sheikhs who support him, not only in his personal way

---

[1] Abraham Haibem—Deputy Prime Minister of Jordan, Suliman Toukan—the Minister of Defence, and Ackman C. L. Hossaing, of the Jordan Foreign Office.

of living, but in his mode of thought. He may be a simple and wholehearted Moslem, but he draws eagerly and wisely on the whole Western system of life, and adapts it to his own purposes—an example which the sheikhs themselves have not yet found it necessary to follow. Thus the contrast between life in the black tents and life in the Basman Palace is sharply marked.

Seeing the sheikhs with the King, however, I did not fail to note that he and they are as one man. They treat him with deference, but they never lose their dignity. They remain free men in whatever company they find themselves; and the Hashemite House is so integral a part of the history of Arabia that the sheikhs have come to regard its head as their personal friend—which, indeed, he is.

The bedouin supporters of King Hussein constitute an armed force, in the literal sense of the term. Whether they have been recruited into the modern Jordan Army, or whether they are still in the desert, they are all armed men. They regard their bullet-belt as part of their dress, and they appear not so much to carry their arms as to wear them; and though their arms are not always new, they are always beautifully kept. A younger son of the Sheikh Mithcal Faiz showed me his gun—of German design—which had belonged to a member of an Israeli patrol before capture in 1946. It was oiled, and cleaned as meticulously as table silver under the supervision of a Victorian butler. Such weapons too become lethal in the hands of their highly skilled owners, of whom about fifty thousand are still nomadic: fifty thousand bedouin Arabs (not counting women and children) from whose tents Hussein can recruit large numbers for his fighting forces, and many of whom prove that the King is not the only crack shot in Jordan.

The place of women in this bedouin world is clearly defined. The sheikhs favour the number of wives the Prophet Mohammed allows—a maximum of four; but they take mistresses from time to time, outside the family circle. Their wives are very well-disciplined, graceful women, often quite fair, and frequently possessed of character and charm. Few of them favour monogamy and regard it as a form of Western hypocrisy designed to make a husband 'unhappy.' These women still uphold the old belief that it is the woman's duty to please her lord. Certainly they appear happy. Their philosophy seems to bestow on them serenity and composure, even dignity.

The bedouin women have escaped the study of trained Western observers almost entirely. Arab men shelter their women and suspect the prying eyes of foreigners; yet my wife was able to have long conversations with bedouin wives, and it surprised her to find that many of them were tall and fair, and mostly unveiled. Cooking, and looking after the tents, and sometimes helping with the animals, occupied most of their time. They were curious about, but not envious of, Western life. They neither smoked nor drank alcohol. The younger ones were full of fun and ready to laugh. None of them, young or old, appeared to doubt, for a moment, the overlordship of their men, any more than the men questioned their allegiance to their sheikh.

Matrimonial differences are very rare among the bedouin. Usually the husband will settle any domestic crisis in his own way by inflicting a just punishment on the recalcitrant wife, or by taking another younger, prettier girl as wife to show his displeasure. But in certain cases the matter is put before the sheikh, who will investigate, consider, and arbitrate.

All the women were interested in Jordanian personalities and a report that the King might marry the Princess Huzina, now at finishing school in Switzerland, intrigued them.

Why are they happy? I think the answer is that they are not frustrated, either in their relationships with their husbands, or in their daily lives. The wind, the rain, the desert are their companions—natural, not artificial, factors in their lives. Perhaps, in their way, they achieve the great happiness that some women secure in a convent. Asked if they would change their lot for a flat in Jerusalem or Amman or Beirut, they laughed, and said, "Certainly not!"

The young King seems to favour monogamy, and there is little doubt that when he weds a Moslem Princess the lady will be his only wife. The change seems inevitable. Whereas monogamy was, until recently, looked upon as shameful, and even ridiculous, for an Eastern monarch, it has now become a symbol of modernity to his people. King Hussein plays this rôle of the modern monarch quite naturally, not only in his domestic life but in his public life too.

Yet however great an appeal the Western way of life may hold for the King, there is little doubt that his future, and that of the new nation he is building up day by day, lies largely in the hands of the men of the desert— his loyal bedouin. Just as the Prophet took to the desert when driven from the towns, so the Hashemite House might revert to the desert to re-group their forces, in an emergency. But they would return. Led by Hussein, they would return to combat, with all their might, the Powers of Darkness—for as such the King regards Communism in all its guises.

7

The King and the Jews

King Hussein, as an Arab leader, has more than once restated the Arab view on the Republic of Israel—namely, that it does not, legally, exist, that a part of Palestine is merely occupied by Jewish forces. But this attitude, having its roots in modern history, is akin to the pleading of lawyers. It is intended to reach the root of the dispute —which it does—and establish a position. It is not designed to procure a solution, either of the Israeli question, or its reverse aspect—the problem of the Arab refugees.

King Hussein is more deeply concerned in this question than any other Arab ruler, if only because his border with the 'State of Israel' is much more extensive than those of other Arab states, and because his Kingdom has given refuge to half a million Arab refugees—five times the number succoured by any other Arab state, and a number equivalent to half the original population of Jordan itself, including the nomadic bedouin. Moreover, as I have pointed out before, the King has granted Jordanian citizenship to every refugee, a gesture without precedent in recent history. These refugees are not stateless. In this respect Jordan's action, in humanity and enlightenment, is far in advance of the post-war policies of France, Britain, the United States, or the Soviet Union.

I will deal separately with the world of the Arab refugees in Jordan, for the question of their loyalty to the King, and their possible integration into the nation, is a fascinating and difficult one that does not directly influence the King's attitude towards Israel.

The King's stand on the Israeli issue has for its foundation the resolution of the United Nations which stated quite clearly that those Arabs who wished to return to their homes should be allowed to do so, and that proper compensation should be paid to those who had suffered damage and loss. In 1948, when it was passed, the resolution was right and just. It is still right and just, but it is no longer convenient.

In order to begin to understand this question it is necessary to know the Jordan-Israeli border, to travel its length, as I did, and become familiar with its strange intricacies and their awful consequences. You can, for instance, motor to the border at Jerusalem, where it splits the city, and you can visit other similar sections at Latrun—where the wine comes from—and at Tulkarm, to the north. And there is a road that leads through Hebron to the border, and beyond to Beersheba. But in order to appreciate the real significance of the border it is necessary to attach oneself to the patrols, to actually tread the border step by step.

The demarcation line which surrounds the entire area, except the southern desert sector which, though not unprotected, is not marked, consists of eight strands of barbed wire stretched over crossed stakes. It is an absolute barrier. The penalty for trying to cross it is death from Israeli and Jordanian bullets—a barrage of fire. The line, which was drawn, not by agreement, but imposed by force on the cessation of the Israeli-Arab war, is capricious in the extreme. It divides villages, farms, municipal facilities, and even families. I came across a dozen families with members on both sides of the border because their land had been split into two sections. In such cases the family is completely broken up. The Israeli members might as well be in China, so far removed are they from their Jordanian members, living perhaps a hundred yards away.

This is the situation that Hussein, as the leader of Jordan, has to grapple with. At the time of writing the situation is explosive. A state of war exists between Israel and all the Arab states. Not a cold war, a war that may become active suddenly, without warning.

The King possesses religious toleration as well as faith. At Christmas 1959, when I was in Amman, he issued a message saying that he felt responsible for the future of the Holy Land, and the places dear to all Christians who were within the Kingdom of Jordan. "It is our duty to protect and preserve these holy places of the Christian faith," he said; and at Christmas he sent a message of goodwill and good cheer to all his people. So when the King tackles the Israeli issue he is not like an inflexible old man bogged down in the past. He is a young man aware that to-morrow is more important than yesterday. In this awareness lies the chief hope of an eventual settlement of the Israeli-Arab dispute.

Certainly this burning question must force Western leaders to take some action very soon. The mandate of the United Nations to care and cater for the refugees expires in 1960. It is inconceivable that half a million people in Jordan, many of them young people, will be

allowed to perish. Yet that is the fate that awaits them if
nothing is done. Slow starvation is their fate, certainly,
if Jordan should have another drought similar to that of
1958–59, when the price of a working camel fell from
eighty to five dinar, and cattle, sheep, goats, and camels
died by the thousand.

King Hussein sees little encouragement from outside
except in a few wise and generous moves that have been
made—for example, the inauguration of Refugee Year
by four young men, including the British runner, Chris
Chataway. But these moves, though they may augment
the funds available for the refugees, will not solve the
Israeli question.

I asked King Hussein if the problem was as intractable
as it seemed. He asked me to discuss the question with
his Foreign Minister, as he feels that this one subject is
so vital, and so complicated, that the less the Arab
leaders say the better. But it was clear that the Minister was expressing the King's own views and,
having spent months on a study of these views, I am
sure that the Israeli-Arab, and especially the Israeli-
Jordan, dispute can be settled only by a radical change
of heart by the Israeli authorities. This is now taking
place.

Although the King takes up what has now become,
after a decade of escapism by the Western Powers,
traditional Arab attitudes on the Israeli question, he is
deeply concerned to reach a settlement.

Jordan does not relish having a long border with a
State with whom, technically, she is at war, nor is it in
Jordan's interest to give succour for ever to thousands of
Palestinian Arabs who wish to return to Palestine. This

brings us to the questions that are never asked about the Palestine impasse:

How many of the Arab refugees would in fact accept compensation in the place of the right to return to their homeland?

How many refugees is Israel prepared to repatriate?

How much compensation is she willing to pay?

To find out just how far the Arabs and the Jews were from a settlement, I asked the Israeli Ambassador in London for his views. He was good enough to put them in writing for me, and made three main points:

1. Please examine the resolution of the U.N. of November 29, 1947, on the partition of Palestine and note the defiance of it by the Arab States, including Jordan. The refugee problem was created by Arab aggression.

2. All the United Nations resolutions stressed the necessity of Arabs and Jews living in peace. The Arab leaders have never made this possible, nor stated its desirability.

3. Israel is ready to compensate. The U.N. resolution requires the Arab States to assist in resettlement. Nothing has been done.

The Ambassador's comments—and he is very close to his Government—might at first sight appear to be a mere reinstatement of a deadlock, but I do not think they are quite that. The outcome seems to be more a plea for co-operation from both sides. I am convinced that handled by the right people, whose disinterestedness is accepted, Arab and Jew can settle their differences. This is not publicly admitted in an Arab state, but I feel that the view should be expressed, nevertheless, in the interest of the Arab states themselves. The simple fact is that the United States would not tolerate the destruction of Israel—and that appears to be the only alternative solution to a settlement—so, sooner or later, a just settlement there must be.

In talks I have had with leaders of public and national opinion it has become clear that the King's problem is not quite as intractable as one might at first imagine. For instance, (a) the number of Arab refugees who would insist on repatriation is hardly likely to be more than half the number now resident outside Palestine; (b) the compensation which Israel would pay, plus a capital sum that the United Nations might pay to avoid its heavy annual refugee bill, would go a long way towards meeting the demands of those Arabs who would accept compensation; (c) Israel would have to revise her ideas on repatriation, making the present suggested quotas much larger.

In other words, this is a human world problem capable of solution. If in the near future new leaders take over in America and Britain it is more than possible that a solution would be arrived at by the Eastern rulers concerned, but if no foreign initiative is taken, including United Nations initiative, then the responsibility of making the first move may rest with the young King of Jordan.

The present situation borders on the farcical. No Arab state will admit any one who has an Israeli visa on their passport. A certificate of faith is necessary to enter Jordan. It does not matter what faith is certified— Christian, Buddhist, Moslem, or Agnostic—but it must not be the Jewish Faith. In so far as the Jewish Faith is part of the Christian tradition, though it may be regarded as an apostasy, these regulations are a strange aftermath of the Arab-Israeli war, in which men of both sides lost their lives for the cause in which they believed.

Among the more strident politicians of Jordan there is a certain amount of anti-Semitism. It is said that the new immigrants to Israel, who are being welcomed by the Israeli Government to the exclusion of the Arabs, the rightful owners of the land, are mostly from Iron Curtain countries, that they are low types of humanity leading a life, in the early months of settlement, not far removed from animals, feeding from troughs, incredibly dirty, with no loyalty, and no decorum. It is felt that these visitors are being deliberately invited to pollute the homes which the Arabs have lost.

So, in a sense, the longer the problem is allowed to remain unsolved, the longer it will last, becoming more difficult as the small State of Israel reaches her human-capacity quota.

There is one other very interesting factor that I noticed when I was the guest of the King's Government in Jordan—the fact that many of the refugee camps appear to a visitor to be becoming suburbs of the city near which they have been erected. I do not doubt that, settlement or no settlement, the Refugee Camp at Amman will in ten years time be part of the city of Amman. Already I saw the signs—a bus service, water and light, the beginning of a shopping street, and I deal with this and other features more fully in Chapter 8, "The King and the Refugees"; but if the Western Powers think that time alone will solve this bitter human calamity that has festered now for a considerable number of years they are mistaken. Only bold, clear thinking and some enlighten-ment will solve it. "Where there is no vision, the people perish." The old biblical saying is as true to-day as when it was first uttered.

The Israeli-Jordan feud can only be settled by a change of heart. Those who have tussled with the bitter and complicated issues of the East-West ideological struggle are in many ways unsuited to bring about a solution of this intensely Arab issue; but it is possible that under Swedish or Indian chairmanship the Arab leaders might respond to proposals made by the Israeli leaders for an overall settlement. This would include:

1. An end to the state of war between Israel and the Arab states that has persisted since 1948.

2. The resettlement and compensation of the Arab refugees on the lines of the United Nations directive at last implemented.

3. The reopening of frontiers long closed.

4. The abandonment by Israel of her greater Israel projects at the expense of her Arab neighbours.

If a settlement could be achieved it would be the greatest advance towards peace made in the last decade, unless the German question is settled meantime. What is going to prove fatal to any negotiations is any attempt on the part of Anglo-American Power politics to guide the course of a settlement to their own advantage. Advantages would accrue in any case to the West. To take one small example—the American firm of Willys, formerly selling jeeps in the Lebanon and in Jordan, has been ousted by firms not having an Israeli account. Fair and equitable trading opportunities in the Middle East for all competitors would be only one minor offshoot of a settlement.

Needless to say, the major benefit of such a settlement

would be the fact that a state of war, endangering the peace of the world, would exist no more between Arab and Jew, and King Hussein has proved, by his restraint and wisdom, that he will play his part in any such move to bring peace and prosperity to Jordan and to her neighbouring Arab states.

8

The King and the Refugees

No account of the life and activities of King Hussein would be complete that did not include an appreciation of the situation created by the Palestinian refugees in Jordan, whose number has been estimated at 545,000 made up, approximately, as follows:

AMMAN (two camps)	107,000
NABLUS (seven camps)	130,000
JERUSALEM (four camps)	85,000
JERICHO (four camps)	94,000
HEBRON (four camps)	87,000
IRBED (one camp)	42,000

The indigenous population of Jordan is about 950,000 so that for every two Jordanians there is one refugee. If one were to create a similar situation in Britain we should have to look after twenty-five million refugees, and the United States would have to care for seventy-five million.

In the anxieties and perplexities of the Arab refugee problem the magnificent rôle played by Jordan under the inspiration of King Hussein is often lost sight of. No country in the world has made a comparable effort. Jordan's neighbours, Egypt, the Lebanon, and Syria, have given refuge to the remaining 400,000 refugees divided between them, but Jordan, the least wealthy of the Arab states at present, has shouldered over half the entire burden. In terms of humanity and compassion alone, setting aside all political questions, the Jordanian effort is unique in the post-war years.

Jordan has allowed this vast horde of refugees to cross her frontiers, has given without charge, the very extensive land necessary to erect their camps, has provided police protection for all the camps, and has assisted U.N.R.W.A. (United Nations Relief and Works Agency) in bringing the main services—light and water—to the camps; and the Jordan Government, as has been acknowledged in United Nations reports for over a decade, has co-operated with U.N.R.W.A. in all matters that relate to this mammoth undertaking.

King Hussein has visited all the camps which have been the target of Soviet and Iraq propaganda against the King and Jordan, and I visited the camps for long periods, making a study of the conditions there. Although Soviet propaganda has constantly asserted that the camps were anxious to rise up and destroy the Government of Jordan, as one senior refugee said, "It would indeed be strange and ungrateful if we were to try to harm the only people apart from U.N.R.W.A. who have helped us."

My own impression is that the camps play very little political part in the life of Jordan. Politics centre round the King, the Prime Minister's office, the High Command, and the Police, in that order. Disbanded political parties are always prone to stage a come-back, and among Jordanian intellectuals—lawyers, in particular—there is always a certain amount of political ferment, not of necessity designed to overthrow the Government, but to introduce, peacefully and gradually, more liberal and democratic concepts.

In order to understand this aspect of the King's responsibilities, and what it is that brings the Secretary-General of the United Nations to Jordan so often, we should know the kind of life a refugee leads.

As an example, let us take the new Amman camp. It must be understood that even to-day the population of the camps is not static. Refugees sign off, having become integrated with the general population to such an extent that they no longer desire camp residence or camp rations. Other new refugees are admitted. The stream never stops. Israeli policies, in particular the Israeli Land Acquisition Act, designed to enable the Government to seize the remaining Arab property in Israel, have ensured that the stream of refugees shall be kept alive. But the influx is small now, for the border, over its demarcated area, is closely guarded.

There is still an infiltration from Syria, and from the Egyptian Sinai peninsular, but, by and large, the refugee population, with all its births and deaths, remains at over half a million. Although births are always recorded, deaths are often not recorded, as the families are anxious not to have their small ration quotas reduced. The dead are often buried secretly—not a difficult matter in the hot, dry sands of Jordan. By practice, this strange community seems to have developed a secret technique for disposing of its dead members. It is a ghoulish aspect of camp life, but one that I found fascinating, if horrible. Speaking of it to Mr Tamimi, a camp official, but formerly a police detective under the British mandate, I was told that practically no deaths are recorded at all now.

As hygiene and nourishment improve, the birth-rate rises fairly rapidly, but the death-rate has almost reached zero as far as the camp records are concerned, so that on paper the refugee problem, far from diminishing is increasing. Furthermore, this extraordinary secrecy that surrounds death in the camps suggests that the medical staff know what is going on; and this brings us to the fact that nearly all camp officials are drawn from the ranks of the refugees themselves, so their loyalties, naturally, are to the refugees, rather than to U.N.R.W.A.

It must be very difficult for the refugees to find out who is about to die, but apparently they are very well-informed, and a shroud descends on the doomed man— and that is the last officialdom hears of him.

The underground nature of these proceedings suggests that in other directions there may be activities in the camps which the outside world never hears of. It may well be that an extensive Communist network operates throughout the camps. It would not be altogether surprising. The Jordan Government has a well-armed police post in each camp, and if there are Communist cells no doubt the Soviet Union has its agents in such posts. Any camp would be a fine refuge for a spy, or ring of spies. The more I studied the enigma of the camps, the more curious I became.

Even now so little is known of the lives of these strange subjects of King Hussein that I give the details of an Admittance Card to the New Amman Camp, followed by certain other details, not before, I think, mentioned in non-technical descriptions of refugee life:

The Admittance Card, which is headed "UNRWA —JORDAN Admittance Card, New Amman Camp," states the ration-card number, the hut number, the family names—head of household, wife, children, dependants, their age, sex, relationship, and whether immunized for small-pox and T.A.B. There is also a column for medical certificates.

The card must bear the signatures of the 'eligibility assistants' and certify that the family are genuine refugees, and the signatures of the delousing officer and the billeting official. It is a human document of extraordinary interest, and I cannot help thinking that instead of descriptive pamphlets written at second hand and used by all the organizations now dedicated to helping the refugees, photos of these cards and of all the other refugee documents would have the effect of bringing home the real life led by the refugees in a far more graphic form.

Tents are now replaced almost entirely by buildings of brick and mud in all the camps. What a family is now allocated—the 'hut'—is usually three metres by three, with no heating or sanitation, but there is public water and sanitation. There are public baths, and special diets for under-nourished children.

It will probably come as a shock to a large number of well-nourished Western readers to know what a refugee receives as rations. This is the diet that the world, so full of new riches, which can afford to spend billions on the hydrogen bomb, can afford to give these people, per month per person.

About 1,500 calories,[1] made up as follows:

    10 kilos of flour.
    5 grammes of sugar.
    500 grammes of rice.
    700 grammes of beans.
    350 grammes of oil.
    Half a kilo of dates and a piece of soap.

In addition to their huts, most families are now granted —again through the generosity of the Jordan Government—a piece of land ten metres by ten, on which they can, themselves, build another room, and, perhaps, a lavatory.

I have gone into the background of life in the camps in some detail, because it is necessary to know at least this much to understand the kind of questions with which King Hussein is constantly having to grapple. He is very much a working King, dealing from day to day with practical, pressing matters, and there are no matters more urgent than those that concern the refugees.

The refugees have a system of Home Rule by which their Elders, or chosen representatives, can speak for them. Often their leaders seek the King's aid. On a visit I paid to the King a group of fifteen of these representatives were calling on him with a detailed list of suggestions and protests. Of course, to a certain extent, it is possible for the King to hand over these matters to a Minister, but this cannot be done to the extent it is done in England.

Here in England the old personal link between the subject and the Sovereign by Petition only survives in

---

[1] Undernourished refugee children have a special diet, better than the above, but less than 25 per cent. of normal requirements.

our antiquated and exclusively expensive legal system, but in the East the link has not been broken—at least, not in Moslem and Buddhist countries. The poorest of the poor have always been allowed to hand in their carefully written prayer to the supreme power, if they can catch the King's eye, or enlist the aid of a kindly Minister. King Hussein feels his personal responsibility for the refugees.

In the meantime funds are running low. Every move by the United Nations, seldom reported in the Western Press, is fully reported in the Jordan Press. Early this year, for instance, under the heading, "U.N. Assembly calls for more funds," *Falastin*, an Amman paper, reported:

> The General Assembly yesterday called upon the Secretary-General, Dr Dag Hammarskjöld, to continue and increase his efforts to procure more funds for the Arab refugees.
>
> The General Assembly adopted a resolution of the Political Committee that members be asked to increase their contributions. U.N.R.W.A. was also called upon to continue its relief and rehabilitation projects.

The United Nations know that in their great task in Jordan they have one ardent and faithful supporter and friend—the King. The Secretary-General has mapped the whole course of development in Jordan with the King's aid and encouragement. One branch of this development, rehabilitation, which until two years ago was showing remarkable progress, though meeting with a lot of refugee opposition on the political grounds that this was accepting the present position as *un fait accompli*, has had to cease entirely through lack of funds.

However detached one tries to be when contemplating

this explosive problem, the fact that rehabilitation has been halted for over two years is something of a disgrace to the United Nations members. If the refugee problem cannot be solved at present at least the initiated efforts to contain it should not have to be dropped.

Although the refugees, in spite of incitement by foreign agencies, form no threat to the established Government of Jordan, other than that provided by a large malcontent society and, possibly, some political fanatics who might be induced to indulge in murder or arson, the refugees dominate one aspect of Jordan relations—her relations with Israel.

The Jordan Government takes its stand on this question by quoting the solemn resolutions of the General Assembly of 1948, 1949, and 1950. The refugees were to be repatriated to live at peace with their neighbours, or they were to be compensated as soon as possible. That was well over ten years ago. The world in effect decided that the Israeli-Arab war was to end, and that peace was to be restored, and the refugees repatriated or compensated.

Nothing was done, and this explains the bitterness and disillusion one meets with in the camps. I recall the things said to me very clearly:

"The British are liars. They do not intend to help the Arabs."

"The Americans are cheats. They pretend to want to help the refugees while in fact they help Israel with guns and money."

"The United Nations is not a really independent body. It is dominated by America and the American South-American satellites. Whenever the Soviet Union puts forward a solution or suggestion the lawyers are set to work to pick holes in it."

"The Western Powers do not care about the refugees. We embarrass them. If they could drown us all to-morrow they would gladly do so—if there was no publicity."

"President Eisenhower is just a sick old soldier who does not understand, and is not told, what is going on."

"The Jews will never have us back if they can help it. Hitler drove them out, and now, with guns in their hands, they have adopted the Hitler methods against us, only worse."

This is the kind of political thinking that permeates the constrained atmosphere of the camps. It is not surprising. I think that as a civilian prisoner of the Japanese for four years I was able to understand the mentality of the refugees, for iron bars are not necessary to make a prison. The camps are free in principle but the hut number and the ration card are the walls of a domination as soul-destroying as prison itself.

There is, I think, little doubt that a school of thought existed among Western politicians which believed that the refugee problem would be solved by time. This is not so, and there are signs that the great camps are tending to become suburbs of the cities near which they are built. I noticed this to a marked extent in Amman and in Jerusalem. There are, too, a number of wealthy refugees who managed to bring enough wealth with them to start business in Jordan, and who, by their skill and industry, have since increased it. Some of these people own the most lavish homes on the hills in residential Amman. They are refugees in name only.

But the real problem remains, and it has never been larger. The Israeli-Arab dispute, on the settlement of which the fate of the refugee seems to depend, will never be settled without the co-operation of the Arab states and with the help of United Nations initiative. In my study of Jordan under King Hussein I became convinced that no progress would be made unless all the parties took as their motto, "To-morrow is more important than yesterday."

Meantime, while prejudice, meanness, and ignorance beset the great human burden and duty which the refugees present, we should at least remember the day-to-day work of two men who live with the situation as an ever-present challenge. One is the Secretary-General of the United Nations, the only man living whose white jeep, with the letters U.N. emblazoned on it, passes quickly and safely over the borders of the Arab states and Israel, and the other is the young King, who has half a million impoverished guests on his hands, to whom, in the best tradition of the Arab Princes, he has extended the hospitality of his Kingdom.

In Arab tradition a guest stays three days—the day of arrival, the day of talk and feasting, the day of planning departure. The refugees are still there. And still the heart and mind of the West is not stirred to positive, constructive action.

9
Commander-in-Chief

In the Constitution of Jordan the relationship of the King to the armed forces is clearly set out: "The King is the Commander-in-Chief of the Navy, Army, and Air Force. He declares war, concludes peace, and signs treaties. The King exercises his jurisdiction by *iradas*."

Most constitutional monarchs hold a similar position but King Hussein, during the six years of his reign, has interpreted his duties as meaning that he should be the inspiration and active partner of his armed forces, knowing his officers and men, visiting them constantly, sharing their lives. In this respect no other living king or head of state can compare with him. He has turned the cold, formal words of the legal Constitution into a pattern of life, making himself the active head of his services, a brother to his officers, the personal Prince of each of his soldiers.

It is, by any standard, an achievement of merit, and it has earned the King a rich reward. In so far as there is stability in the Near East, in so far as the borders are respected—the Egyptian border, the Israeli border, the Lebanese, Syrian, and Iraq borders—this is due to a great extent to the simple abiding loyalty of the Jordan Army to their King.

Many observers think that there are only two armies in the whole area that are effective fighting forces: the

G

Jordan Army and the Israeli forces. These armies face
each other over a long border. Many miles of the border
are closely guarded. Many miles of desert are lightly
patrolled. In the middle of this quick-silver area prone to
political explosion the Jordan Army and Air Force
stand like a rock, a warning to any who might be
tempted to embark on aggression.

With the King's permission and the active help of his
officers, I spent weeks with the modern Jordan Army,
meeting the commanding officers. It was a revealing
experience, and I still have my pass into the Zerqa Army
Headquarters.

The sections of the Army which King Hussein has
taken the most active interest in are the Royal Jordanian
Air Force, the Royal Military Academy, the Royal
Artillery, and the Royal Armoured Corps; and of these,
the King's personal qualifications as a pilot, including
the pilotage of jet aircraft, make his interest in the Air
Force an absorbing one.

It is difficult to realize how new and modern the
Jordanian Air Force is. It was, in fact, ten years old in
1959. In 1949 three aircraft were purchased, and
candidates were chosen and flown to the United Kingdom
for training as pilots and technicians. From this very
modest start, the present completely modern force has
been developed during the last six years, under King
Hussein, at a much accelerated pace.

In 1955 the Arab Legion Air Force was renamed the
Royal Jordanian Air Force, and the first jet fighters
appeared streaking across the indigo sky above Amman.

In 1959, with the King's approval, twelve of the most
modern Hunter jet fighters were purchased from

Britain with funds provided by American aid. These superb aircraft are now lined up in their sheds, in the military section of Amman airport, in a state of instant readiness. Their pilots, all Jordanians, maintain the highest pitch of training, and the King, when in Amman, has on several occasions joined his officers in exercises, piloting one of the planes.

The King flies his jets with expertness. When his mother, Queen Zayn, was returning to Amman from a visit abroad, the King, piloting his own jet, went out to meet her, accompanied her plane for some miles, then, at the last minute, raced ahead, to be waiting to receive her as she herself stepped from the slower civil aircraft.

When talking to the King it is quite obvious that he believes that constitutional monarchy means personal leadership. The King has to do everything, if possible, better than the next man. That is his creed, and in the matter of his Air Force he has been able to put it into practice convincingly.

In special hangars on Amman airport there are some interesting aircraft. As well as the new Hunters, to be supplemented by a more modern Mark, are the older fighters and bombers, and the King's two personal aircraft emblazoned with the arms of his House. One is the comfortable but slow Moth plane, in which the King was attacked over Syrian territory, and in which he escaped only by flying out at tree-top level towards the Jordan border after making a dummy run as if to land, in compliance with 'orders' from Damascus. Next to this plane is housed the new Beech aircraft that the King uses now. It is capable of between 250 and 300 miles per hour. I inspected this plane. The seating is modern and very comfortable The seats face the engine, the passengers sitting side by side, as in a car. This aircraft also carries very clearly on both panels the arms of Jordan. It is quite certain that these planes are known and instantly recognized by all Israeli, Egyptian, and Syrian pilots, as they would be by the Iraq Air Force. The point may not be without interest if the King makes more flights in his personal plane. However, it is more likely that on such occasions his plane would be accompanied by the Hunter jet escort. He ordered such an escort to accompany his brother, the Crown Prince Mohammed, leaving for a foreign tour.

When the King departed on his recent world tour he left by Saudi Arabia, and returned by way of Turkey for his talks with the Shah, in Teheran. He did not use the Syrian air passage again, not wishing to invite United Arab Republic treachery.

Whether the renewal of diplomatic relations between Jordan and the United Arab Republic means that the King's air trips can return to normalcy remains to be seen.

The King visited the Hunter jet factory in Britain, and examined with great care the improvements made during twenty-four months. It seems certain that Jordan will order more of these magnificent planes that have advantages over the best Soviet and United States fighters, including a very much sharper manoeuvrability.

The Jordan Air Force is building itself up rapidly, and there is an obvious attempt to keep on a parity both with Egypt and with Israel. The quality of the Jordanian pilots is at least as good as either of these neighbours can provide.

Amman airport serves both civil and military needs.

It is sufficiently extensive for future development. The Jordan bombers have recently been fitted with new armour and more modern bombs. The King's interest in his Air Force has had results. Certainly the Jordan Air Force is in a position now to prevent another Syrian incident. The Hunter is a valuable escort plane as well as a deadly fighter. With such protection no Eastern air force is likely to be so rash as to interfere again with the King's progress by plane in and out of Jordan. Incidentally, these Hunters, with the aid of an easily fitted additional petrol tank, can reach Malta—a tribute to the extended range of the newest jet planes.

The rapid development of his Air Force, is almost a daily concern of the King's, so the Royal Jordanian Air Force is "Royal" not only in name but in fact.

The Royal Armoured Corps, which started in 1953 with a single Tank regiment, has developed under Hussein's personal encouragement into a hard-hitting, mobile force, capable, in conjunction with the other Army units, of defending Jordan against any invasion by neighbours.

The Armoured Corps is typical, in its development, of the other armed services. Until 1956 it was largely British-officered and entirely British-trained. It is now exclusively officered by Jordanians, but still the training is partly foreign—in the United Kingdom and Pakistan. When it does take place in Jordan, then it is conducted by men who, in their turn, have been trained abroad.

A very complete modernization of the Tank Corps was overdue and is under way. When it is completed the Royal Armoured Corps of Jordan will be the most modern in the Near East. The new equipment comes from Britain and America. No Russian equipment is accepted by the Jordan armed forces. There is, in fact, no Soviet Embassy in Amman, and the Chinese Embassy is that of the Chiang Kai-Shek Government at Formosa.

The Royal Artillery, the Jordanian 'gunners,' are proud of the fact that the King gave them the title of 'Royal' soon after he ascended the throne, before other branches of the Army were so honoured. Field and heavy artillery and mobile anti-aircraft units are included. Hussein visits the Royal Artillery on manœuvres, and makes his own notes of the accuracy and proficiency of this vital branch of the Jordan Army, so again the personal imprint of the King is apparent.

Perhaps the most revealing branch of the Jordan Army, however, is the Royal Military Academy, that now takes in some two hundred Murashah (cadets), who have the status of officers but are not yet commissioned. I watched these young men at work. Many of them came from the black tents of the Beni Sakhr bedouin. Dark, wiry, alert, tough, they seemed to be ideal officer material; and that is the view of King Hussein. "They have great initiative, are loyal, they can live hard, they are brave and disciplined." In these words the King showed his pride in his young officers-to-be.

To appreciate how much the modern Jordan Army owes to Hussein and his House, it is necessary to remember that the Jordan Army is the outgrowth of the Arab Legion, which was formed after the First World War, and largely officered by Arab officers who had served under the Turks. The first Arab revolt, that led to the present resurgent Arab nationalism, was inspired by Faisal and Lawrence. The Sharifian family rode high in victory, to Beirut, to Amman, to Damascus, and to Baghdad; but in Jordan the Arab Legion continued to be financed, and partly officered, by Britain.

The reign of King Hussein, by no accident, has coincided with the growth of the new Jordan Army as a 100 per cent. Jordanian force, and the King has achieved this without sacrificing the discipline and tradition which the Army inherited from its British sponsors. This is a real achievement. It would have been very natural, in so far as foreign aid was needed at all, to turn to other sources, just to show that the period of 'tutelage' was a thing of the past. This was not done. The political and social era of Glubb Pasha is as dead as the Queen of Sheba, but the spirit and outlook and first-class standards of the highly trained professional soldier, as embodied in General Glubb himself, survive to a remarkable extent throughout the Jordan Army.

The King said to me, "See for yourself. Form your own opinion." And I carried out this command.

Accompanied by Lieutenant Akram Zaki, attached to Jordanian Army Headquarters—and studying aerial photography—I visited the entire Army day after day. Constantly I was reminded of the King's interest, and constantly the tradition of the Arab Legion came through the new, modernized and wholly Jordanian force.

In a country where the drinking of coffee, both Turkish and bedouin, is a social rite and indispensable, the Jordan Army drinks tea, so the visiting Englishman feels quite at home. The scrupulously cared for pebble paths that lead to each Army Headquarters hut are lined with whitewashed stones. The great wooden signs are painted as carefully and as graphically with letters and the regimental emblem as if they were decorating Aldershot or Tidworth. Moreover, the Jordanian officers are as British in outlook as the officers of the crack regiments of India and Pakistan, yet their manner and speech do not portend that they are not good, even fervid, nationalists, in the best meaning of the word.

It is a known fact that many Eastern countries tend to adopt a general view of life similar to those of certain nations of the West. For example, although the spiritual home of the Lebanon is Arab, the Arabian viewpoint bears a notable resemblance to that of Paris; the Philippines may be indigenous, but no one doubts that Manila looks towards Washington; and in Amman, and certainly in the Jordan Army, the Western influence derives from London—or, at least, from London and Washington together. In the East it is the Pakistani and Saudi Arabian attitudes towards life which inspire the warmest sympathy in the people of Jordan.

The Jordan Army has its full complement of branches, even down to the inclusion of a very smart band, one section of which wears the kilt. I came across this band playing in a village square near the Israeli frontier, on a feast-day, surrounded by all the villagers, watching and listening, and it made a brave sight. It was this same band which came to Britain for the coronation of Queen Elizabeth II, when the splendour of its members, together with the dazzling perfection of their drill, made a vivid impression.

Naturally, the Jordan soldier desires to demonstrate his courage in the field, because only in battle can his martial qualities be tested to the full; but laudable as this wish to prove his mettle may be, it is to be hoped devoutly that the Near East may not be subject to the scourge of war. If this hope is not fulfilled, however, and if, in the future, Jordan suffers attack, then the brunt of the fierce onslaught of the first crucial twenty-four hours will be borne by the Jordanian Army—until they are joined by their allies. In such an event we may be confident that the young Hussein will be there with his troops, putting into practice his code of personal leader-ship—that integral part of the kingship to which his whole life is dedicated.

Describing a review of his troops by King Abdullah, General Glubb, in a passage of great simplicity and sincerity, evokes the spirit of the Jordan Army—not only the Jordan Army of his own day, but of to-day: "Thousands of young men passed the saluting base where I stood behind the King. They went by with their heads high and their eyes shining, but not a muscle of their faces moved. I knew what was in their minds. They were showing the world what Arab soldiers could do."

Only in the event of an attack on Jordan will the world feel the full impact, and realize the whole meaning, of General Glubb's unforgettable evocation.

IO

The King and Communism

In order to understand King Hussein's attitude towards Communism, both the international variety and its Jordanian progeny, it is useful to realize how the average Arab regards politics and Western political ideology. The King is by no means an average Jordanian, but in his attitudes he reflects with remarkable fidelity the national feeling.

Political parties in the Arab states, in their present form, only really came into being ten years ago, with the end of the mandates. Under the Ottoman Empire political parties were the one capital crime, for they were suspect of sedition; and even under the British and French mandates political parties—to put it mildly—were not encouraged. There was always the answer, "We are not here as conquerors. The United Nations has entrusted the administration to us for a limited period. After that what you do is your own affair." Present-day Arab distrust of the United Nations stems largely from the U.N. sponsorship of the mandates.

It is true that to some Arabs the period of the mandate now appears, in nostalgic reflection, as a Golden Age of comparative prosperity, but under the mandates there was little political liberty as opposed to well-defined and protected personal liberty.

Into this virgin field that had lain fallow for four

centuries Western and Soviet political ideas began to percolate, in 1946, and very soon the trickle had become a torrent; but the impact did not come from one nation. It came from four—Britain, the United States, the Soviet Union, and France. The political subtleties of each country were lost in the speed of the transfusion, so one result was that the distinction between Communism and Socialism virtually disappeared. To the Jordanian, undoubtedly the Imperialism of Mr Hugh Gaitskell and the modified Socialism of Mr R. A. Butler are incomprehensible. "This is a special British game," they say. "The British have always loved foxes, and this sport of the Labour man dressed in ermine, and the Tory dressed in rags, is part of the British love of red herrings." It makes no impact at all. Likewise the Republican-Democrat tussle in the United States, and the fact that President Eisenhower, a Republican, tolerates a Democratic Senate, is regarded as mildly lunatic. "All it amounts to is that there are two sides, who have agreed to share the spoils of office by changing the regime every few years."

The only great distinction that does make itself apparent to the Jordanians is the one between the wealthy, who, by and large, want to retain the existing order, and the poor, who want to change it.

On the one hand, they see the Communists, who appear to favour a new world order, and on the other, the ultra-traditionalists, among whom they would lump General de Gaulle, President Eisenhower, the American Democratic Party, the British Labour Party—especially its present Shadow Cabinet—and Dr Adenauer, the indestructible old German. "These people don't really want to change anything. Of course they pretend to be in favour of progress. They have to be, for it will take place whether they like it or not."

To some extent Jordanian political parties are themselves to blame for the blotting out of any real distinction in their own minds between Communism and Socialism. For they have openly referred to revolutionary and evolutionary Socialism. But to appreciate fully the situation that confronts the King, let us examine the parties returned to power at the last elections, which any Jordanian intellectual regards as 'free.'

In this election, held after the departure of General Glubb, the following parties returned the members to the House of Representatives in the numbers given below:

Party	Number of seats
Communist Party	3
Baath Party	2
National Socialist Party	9
Arab Constitutional Party	1
Tahrir Party	1
Moslem Brotherhood Party	4
Independents and Liberals	20
	40

Here are the Jordanian views of what these parties represent:

Communist Party: its motto is National Freedom (shades of Hungary!) and it is supported in Jordan chiefly because many people believe that Russia will help Jordan to obliterate the State of Israel. As most of the people of Jordan are very poor, they could not be worse off under Communism, but might be better off. There is no dread of a world war. The clash of ideologies between the West and Russia is said to stem from commercial greed and jealousy.

It has been possible for the Soviet Union to gain a solid position of prestige and power in the Middle and Near East for the following reasons:

1. The Soviet Union has never had 'imperialistic' power in the Middle East. She was the traditional enemy of Turkey, the country that ruled all the Arab states, absolutely.

2. When the World Bank decided to withdraw funds for President Nasser's Aswan Dam Project, Nasser turned to the U.S.S.R. The Soviet Union helped with long term credits and technicians.

3. The U.S.S.R. is regarded by many Near-Eastern intellectuals as the only genuinely Socialist State.

4. The fact that America dislikes and distrusts the Soviet Union adds enormously to U.S.S.R. prestige and appeal to Left-wing politicians.

5. Although the Soviet Government has never declared its support for a policy of crushing Israel, it is felt to be more sympathetic to Arab aspirations than Britain or the United States.

6. The fact that all Soviet contacts are denied in certain Arab countries—for instance, there is no Soviet Embassy in Amman—tends to make Jordanian Socialists think that there is a peculiar attraction in Soviet contacts, though, in fact, the average Jordanian is not at all inclined to Communism, which he regards as an evil thing that would destroy his faith, kill his King, subvert

his country. Moreover, all overt Communists in Jordan are very soon put in prison. The Government has an efficient system of espionage, and security is strict.

Baath Party: a revolutionary Socialist Party that aims at a United Arab nation that would destroy Israel, and thus recover the 'lost lands.' The new Arab super-state would scrap the existing economic and class orders, and introduce basic Socialism. Arab oil would be Arab owned. Relations with France would be severed, French-dominated countries assisted. When I was informed of these aims I had the strong impression that the Baath Party, in the unlikely event of its ever being able to form a majority Government in Jordan, would make itself felt in Washington, London, Paris, and elsewhere.

National Socialist Party: this Party has many of the same aims as the Baath Party, but its methods are quite different. This is a Party of radical intellectuals, with a large following both in the town and country districts of Jordan. It aims at a United Arab State, but, until that can be achieved, greater racial, political, and economic unity between the Arab states is to be encouraged, an Arab *bloc,* or Arab Club, with no foreign members, is to replace the hated Baghdad Pact.

The elimination of Israel is asserted to be essential but, again, one has the impression that if that could not be achieved this Party would not be adverse to negotiation to that end.

The existing economic, religious, and social order is to be changed, eventually, but in the meantime the public is to be educated by lectures and policy pamphlets. Readers will recognize old familiar characteristics in the Jordanian National Socialist Party. Probably in office some of the policies would undergo a trimming process. For instance, would this Party be ready to scrap American and British aid? It was tried once. The Arab states swore to support Jordan with funds, but, as we have seen, the promise was kept for one instalment only.

The National Socialists admit that in Foreign Affairs they are not so radical as the Baath Party, and it would be safe to assume that as they have rather more likelihood of yielding or influencing power they are correspondingly more responsible.

Arab Constitutional Party: this Party has not allowed its small representation to prevent it from stating its aims with great particularity. These aims are:

1. To adopt from other nations those discoveries that make a nation powerful.

2. To revive Arab dominion as achieved under the Sharif Hussein.

3. To protect Arab unity and liberty.

4. To conquer Israel.

5. To increase production and raise the standard of living.

6. To guarantee a minimum wage for city and country workers.

7. Absolute Arab co-operation. Friendship with all nations on a basis of absolute equality (this does not, of course, include friendship with the unrecognized State of Israel).

Islamic Tahrir Party: this is not a very influential group, but interesting. The aim of the Party is to revive— presumably by conquest—the great days of the Moslem Empire, an Empire which will include not only Moslem states in Arabia but those outside, with Moslem majorities, such as Pakistan, Indonesia, and perhaps portions of the Soviet Union!

Most Jordanians regard the aims of this Party as being far removed from present-day reality, but the fact that it has followers at all in Jordan, and is not 'laughed out of Court,' is significant and fascinating.

In the great new Islamic Empire, which would, of course, absorb Jewish-occupied territory, Mecca and Medina would be sacred capitals, and the sword and green flag of the Prophet would reign over 150,000,000 Moslems.

The Islamic Tahrir Party represents a dream that has never quite faded, the dream that one day Islam would regain her old greatness, but, from my observation, I do not think that young Jordanian political thinkers are seriously moving in this direction. The Party is a brave gesture rather than a phase of practical politics.

Moslem Brotherhood Party: this Party, whose professed aims differ very little from the Islamic Tahrir Party, is more successful, perhaps because it is better organized. Its members oppose Communism as being a faith opposed to Islam, and the fact that they feel this to be deeply true may indicate that this belief is shared by many outside politics in Jordan. Islam is essentially the faith of a free man, highly individualistic, whose ego and liberties must not be overridden by any form of bureaucracy. Communism and Islam are opposites. There may be an attraction of opposites, but in Jordan Communism is realized to be a menace, perhaps more dangerous than the more popular butts of Imperialism and Colonialism, which, the Jordanians realize, are fast disappearing of their own accord.

The royal palace at Amman
The flag is at half-mast for the late King Faisal

By courtesy of Studio Angelo

King Hussein with the late King Faisal

(Above) King Hu.
boards his jet figr
Associated Press Phe

King Hussein a.
glider pilot
By courtesy of Studio A

(Below) B.O.A.
Comet 4 in flig.
between London A.
and Jordan
By courtesy of B.O.A.

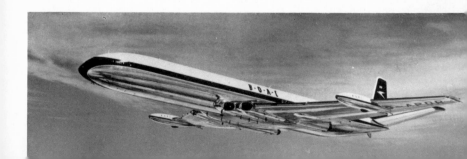

I had the strong impression that the passing of Imperialism was regretted by some Jordanians if only because it formed a wonderful rallying point to unite those who might not be brought together by any other challenge.

These were the parties returned to power in Jordan, in 1956. On the face of it they appear to have a Socialist, not a Communist, trend. But the Jordanians, or many of them, say that there is no essential difference between Communism and Socialism on the economic side, and this is true. Ultimately Socialism and Communism must coincide. The economic life of the nation is taken out of private enterprise and placed under public ownership and control.

In one respect the Arab peoples see clearly something which we are apt to lose sight of: that is the similarity between Communism, as practised in the Soviet Union, and Nazism, as practised under Hitler, for it is the administrative, or executive, aspect of Russian Communism, not its economic doctrine, that makes it repulsive to free men. In the Soviet Union, as in Hitler's Germany, no real opposition is allowed. Under both systems the individual may be arrested and tortured by the secret police at the caprice of the Government. In Britain we sometimes do not see this clearly. Perhaps our admiration for the Red Army's fight against Hitler in the last war, and a realization that America and Britain both owe their present independence and freedom to that heroic campaign as much as to their own great efforts, has hidden this truth from us.

In some ways Western events are seen with great clarity in Jordan. One of the curious features is that no one is concerned by the prospect of a hydrogen war. "It's up to you," they say. "If you are so mad as to start it we shall all perish any way. There is nothing we can do about it. We are more concerned with present actualities than with this monstrous nightmare of yours."

The Parliament based on the parties I have indicated above, led by the Prime Minister, Suliman Nabulsi, issued a Ministerial Statement, and it is interesting to note that, faced now with responsibility and with contact with the Palace, careful and moderate words were chosen to express their views.

In foreign affairs all trace of Western domination was to be removed. In domestic affairs individual liberty was to be secured by a Press Law, a Public Meetings Law, an Electoral and Municipalities Law. The Army Law was to be revised, and national service, as opposed to bedouin recruitment, imposed. The bedouin tribes were to be "helped," and eventually their nomad status would be changed.

On the face of it this appears a mildly radical programme, but in effect it was disastrous for Jordan. The substitution of the Arab states for Britain as a source of annual subsidy ended very quickly in the Arab states defaulting and Jordan being left stranded. The laws on personal liberties led to wholesale rioting in Amman and Jerusalem, which could not be stopped without bloodshed, while the design of the Government on the Army struck at the root of the Royal power, at present the only stable factor in Jordan national life.

The 1956 elections were a tragic lesson for the Jordan people. Those who led them read with pride the solemn undertaking of the sister Arab states to support Jordan.

It was contained in four brief articles, and there could be no doubt as to its meaning.

Article I referred to that cherished conception, "the Arab State," and stated that unity between Arab states was essential to achieve this.

Article II stated that the Egyptian, Syrian, and Saudi Arabian Governments would pay twelve and a half million pounds a year to Jordan.

Article III stated that the Government of Jordan would contribute its armed forces for the cause of Arab unity.

Article IV stated that the agreement would remain in force for ten years and would replace the subsidy of the English.

Four years later these promises were realized by the Jordanians not to be worth the paper they were written on. It was the gravest blow to the aspirations of the reformers. The public could not but realize that on this essential matter the sister Arab states had let down Jordan. Perhaps the King had been right after all when he said that no one could ever help the Jordanian people as they could help themselves.

The predicament in which Jordan then found herself was an unhappy one. To return so quickly to Britain after the breach was unthinkable. It was to Washington that the new Government made its first approach. The State Department and the President gave a favourable answer. For the time being the economic front was saved from collapse.

Then a new anxiety arose. It is true that in the days of Glubb Pasha English ways had permeated a certain class in Jordan, in the Army more than in civilian life, but since the foundation of the new, independent Jordan, Britain had never cracked the whip. There is a saying in the East that one should choose one's creditor with care, and the Jordanians soon discovered that American aid had several strong strings attached to it. Worse than this, because more obvious to the people, everything was 'packaged' in an American, not in an Arab, way. The importance of the right presentation of help was not understood in Washington—though, as we have seen, it was very well understood in Amman by the American diplomatic Mission. Now the lesson is being learnt.

Within months an explosive situation arose in Jordan. The King assumed direct power again. Distinctions became simple, realistic. Being shown over the Parliament building, I asked my guide where the Opposition sat. He thought a moment. "Well," he replied, "the trouble-makers sit over there." Jordan was once more firmly in the hands of King Hussein, his Prime Minister, and his Chief of Staff.

I I

The King and the West

The position of Jordan in its relation to the West is a real
test of the statecraft of King Hussein. In his first two
years as ruler he certainly had much to learn of international relationships. He still has. The King's absorption,
until recently, with security and the internal struggle in
Jordan did not give him time to study as closely as he
now does the foreign news and the trends in foreign
affairs. Several Left-wing Jordanian politicians com-
plained to me about this. They said that certain members
of the Royal family, the Crown Prince, and the Sharif
Nasir thought only of the safety of the King's person. If
this was so it was a very natural preoccupation. Even
though Iraq, before the revolution, was considered to be
more stable than Jordan, and even though King Faisal
had the love and respect of the average Iraqi, who still
reveres his memory, this did not prevent the appalling
butchering of the Royal family. If those round Hussein
who have his interests at heart seem to think that the
future of Jordan is bound up with the King's personal
safety, the answer must be that if King Faisal were now
ruling Iraq would not be lurching towards Communism,
and Baghdad would not be the scene of the most revolting
political trials in recent Near Eastern history.

Now Jordan is moving out of the tight world of
intrigue, counter-intrigue, and insecurity. The nightmare

appears to be all but over, and the King and his Ministers have turned to the West to assure Jordan's future.

Since his recent world tour, that included highly successful visits to Washington and London, it is clear that King Hussein has established valuable friendships in both the greatest Western capitals. There is no doubt that the new understanding arrived at will be honoured when, as seems possible, a Democratic administration takes over in the United States, and should a Labour Government be elected in Britain. The King must feel that he has rendered himself and his country a great service.

This new understanding, and the concrete guarantees that go with it, should not blind us to the kind of public opinion that King Hussein has to grapple with in Jordan. We cannot too quickly realize that, like other Arab states, Jordan rejects the American and British way of life. She prefers her own way. Our religion, our commercial practices, our social pattern, even our form of Government, are not to the Jordanian taste, and they never will be.

If, as seems to be indicated, we are going to spend more money on 'information' or propaganda in Jordan at least let it be a two-way traffic so that we can benefit by Islamic culture, just as they may benefit by our pseudo-Christian culture. On this basis of absolute equality the Jordanians are interested in exchanging ideas with us. But to be only at the receiving end of a constant barrage of persuasion seems to them to be a one-sided arrangement.

In relation to Britain the King has a very provocative history to bear in mind. Until the departure of General

Glubb, Jordan was dominated, militarily, by Britain. The Arab Legion was trained by British officers and financially controlled by Britain. In the time of King Abdullah it is fair to say that the British were not resented, but two developments—the creation of the State of Israel and the disastrous British attack on Egypt, represented to Arab states as a great victory by President Nasser over the combined Imperial might of Britain, France, and the Jews—have changed this. The position is—to put it bluntly—that Britain is out of Jordan except as an equal, an ally, and a friend.

The history of Britain's close friendship with France—the Sykes-Picot Agreement, the de Gaulle-Lyttleton Agreement—have made the Jordanian public regard Britain and France as birds of a feather, the bird being a very imperialistic eagle. Against this background we should regard the King's present plans for closer co-ordination with the West. His new Prime Minister, the bluff, forthright Haaza Pasha Majali, is perhaps more openly pro-Western than the King himself, but both Prime Minister and King have to carry with them the preponderating opinion of the Jordan people. It is because this is not always realized in the West that our relations with Jordan are sometimes difficult.

The United States has escaped, in Jordanian eyes, much of the stigma that attaches to the Imperialism of Britain and France, though there is a growing feeling that the American Government has developed an Imperialism as dangerous, if more insinuating; but, still, in the main the United States is not regarded in the same light as Britain, and certainly not in the same light as France. It is an odd feature of the Near-Eastern scene that the

French, who are in many ways a more civilized and charming race than either of the Anglo-Saxon countries, should have contrived to become so hated by the Arab states.

American aid to Israel, on the other hand, is hotly resented in Jordan. I quote a well-known politician in Amman. "Israel is ready to fight with American aid. She has launched great projects with American money. It takes dollars to buy American ammunition like that found at Nahhalin and Kybaya, after the Israeli murderers had withdrawn. America is feeding her child, Israel, and making no effort to discipline her, as the frontier attacks show."

The King has taken it upon himself to pursue a foreign policy that is much in advance of the one that the average Jordanian would acknowledge. As the King looks at the map he thinks that this is essential to Jordan's future. To his south he has Egypt—a scheming rival; to the north is Syria—now part of Nasser's United Arab Republic. If Jordan fell Nasser's power in the Near East would be without serious challenge. From Turkey to Cairo Nasser's writ would run. Israel would be encircled, not by three Arab states, but—if we leave out the short Lebanese frontier—by one. War would be brought a great deal nearer.

The King has the capacity for thinking in terms of to-morrow. He sees that while Jordan is getting on her feet she will need strong friends. Now she has them, and for this the Jordanian Government and people have to thank the boldness and statecraft of their King and his Prime Minister.

The new links between Jordan and the West make it of

interest to see the ways in which the King has encouraged Anglo-American co-operation in Jordan.

In order to place Jordan on her feet economically and commercially, the King's Government negotiated loans with Britain as follows, with repayment agreements as set out here:

BRITISH DEVELOPMENT LOANS TO JORDAN

Loan made in	Amount £	Repayable starting in	Number of Instalments
1950	1,000,000	1956	15
1952–53	1,500,000	1959	15
1953–54	500,000		
1954–55	1,600,000	1960	15
1955–56	1,750,000	1961	15
1956–57	1,120,000	1962	15
1957–58	500,000	1963	10
1958–59	630,000	1964	10

Total £8,600,000

The sums payable in Jordanian dinars by Jordan, in repayment of these loans, will be as follows:

	JD (Approx.)		JD (Approx.)
1956–58	67,000 annually	1964–69	612,000 annually
1959	200,000	1970–72	545,000 annually
1960	307,000	1973	495,000
1961	424,000	1974	299,000
1962	499,000	1975	192,000
1963	549,000	1976	75,000

The United States has now become the chief supporter of Jordan's finances. I quote from the official figures: "The first American aid to Jordan in 1954 amounted to 1,400,000 dollars. In June of that year an economic aid agreement was signed for 8,000,000 dollars. In November the Jordan Development Board announced a five-year plan of development in industry and communications at the cost of 200,000,000 dollars embracing 274 projects."

This is obviously an attempt to put Jordan on her feet firmly in the shortest possible time; and the King has looked to the two great Western allies for this aid.

It is an open secret that Soviet aid would have been forthcoming at any time, on very advantageous terms, and without obvious political strings attached. Such approaches have always been declined by Jordan. The King has sought to ensure the future of his people by foreign aid from that quarter where, he believes, no designs are entertained that would endanger the liberty of his people, or the national sovereignty of Jordan; but he has not been afraid to put his cards on the table and enter into heavy commitments to the West.

If we take into account American "Point Four" aid to Jordan, the 1959 British aid and equipment, the British influence in the Jordan market, and the influence exercised on the spot by the Anglo-American representatives acting for their Governments, it is obvious that the King is willing to link Jordan firmly to the West, as opposed to Soviet Russia, but he has retained a completely free hand in relation both to Israel and the other Arab states.

This attitude has taken personal courage of a very

direct kind. For three months the Soviet Press threatened that the steps being taken by the King might lead to his assassination. He was told in so many words by the Iraq Press, that he would be murdered as his cousin King Faisal had been murdered. It is seldom that civilized states, having engineered one mass murder, will openly threaten to repeat the crime, but we may be sure that the names of the Baghdad murderers are known, and that one day they will be brought to justice. In the meantime it would be more fitting if those who had a hand in that ghastly outrage, which sank to the lowest human depravity, ceased to make threats against other members of the Hashemite House.

At least we can be glad that such threats have no effect on the morale of the young King. He goes about his daily duties fearlessly and openly, trusting that his friends will support him if he needs support, but the indications are that at present he is well able to look after himself. Incidentally, anyone who is bold enough to make an attempt on the King's life is going to get a very short subsequent life indeed. The Arab Legion soldiers who protect the King would shoot dead any attacker in a matter of seconds.

The King has given clear indications of his own conception of Jordanian interest in other ways. The fact that Jordan is in the sterling area enables the dinar to maintain a parity with the pound, and the recent strength of the pound sterling throughout the world has been reflected in the strength of the dinar.

The King gives his keen support to every new project that may add to the wealth of his people. Although an upholder of Islam and a protector of the still nomadic bedouin, King Hussein sees that the future of Jordan lies in her industry. Every new project interests him, and he follows through his initial interest, seeing that the project gets the support and patronage it deserves.

A petroleum refinery, using crude oil from the Saudi-Arabian pipeline, which crosses Jordan with a capacity of 150,000 tons a year, is one of the major projects. The owners of the oil would pay for the privilege of crossing Jordan territory in oil instead of cash. A sugar refinery, a new brewery, and a textile mill are all planned, as well as a phosphate factory on a very much enlarged scale. In each of these projects, which it is proposed to finance with the 200,000,000 dollars to be invested by the United States in Jordan, the King takes an interest.

The oil-drilling project of the American Phillips Company, however, has, perhaps, the King's most enthusiastic support. It happened that before I discussed this matter with him I was handed in Britain a document dealing with the secret mineral wealth of Jordan, un-exploited in the days of the mandate. The document was never published, but was compiled by experts in this field. The allegation is made that the British oil interests, as a matter of policy, were opposed to the development of Jordan oil. Very detailed and convincing figures are given in this document, still in my possession, of the location of oil and mineral wealth in Jordan, with estimates of the amount and quality of each locality.

I did not mention to the King that I possessed this information during my talk with him, but asked him whether—three attempts made by the Phillips Company to find oil having failed—there was no real hope. He replied that he thought there was great hope. "Often they drill up to a dozen times before they meet with success."

There can, I think, be little doubt of Jordan's great potential mineral wealth. Certainly applications for concessions continue to reach the King and his Government.

The King studies each offer made, and his concern with the essential financial aspect of Jordan's development has made him a keen businessman.

These are but some of the ways in which King Hussein has reached out to the West to bring the Jordan people through the period of poverty through which they have been passing for over a thousand years. Any wealth that may be brought to Jordan is the King's concern.

I suggested to the King that the tourist traffic could be greatly enlarged, and he agreed that this could be done, asking for suggestions. I suggested a small tourist office in London and another in New York, with very small staffs. Consulates, I explained, however willing, cannot do the work that a tourist agency can do. Moreover, other agents acting for a country other than their own will always try to sell their own country first.

The King was quick to seize on the implications of this, asking for the approximate tourist figures and monetary value of the main tourist countries, and the methods employed.

I ventured to make this comment. "It is an ideal way of making money. They bring their dollars or sterling into the country. They spend it here—and they go."

The King smiled when I said this. Some foreigners have been reluctant to leave Jordan.

The energetic Director of Tourism in Jordan gave me

the impressive list of the steps already taken to make Jordan a tourist centre, but, I am sure, with money, the trade can be trebled.

As the King pointed out, Jordan, the Holy Land, has scenes to offer that no country can rival: Jerusalem, with the Via Dolorosa, the Temple of Herod, the Church of the Nativity, the Mount of Olives—the city of Christ that brings His life back vividly and convincingly; Jerash, the fabulous, complete Roman city; and Petra, the rose-red secret city that has defied time.

Yes, King Hussein looks to the West, to Britain, the United States, to Germany, Scandinavia, and Switzerland, to Italy, and to all the world to come to Jordan and see for themselves. I can add that it is an unforgettable experience.

12
Royal Tours

King Hussein has always been acutely aware that Jordan cannot live alone. Not only does this apply to finance; it is true of support and friendship. Unfortunately, in her early years, the young Kingdom has had bitter enemies, the chief being the Soviet Union and the new State of Israel, aided and abetted by Western observers prejudiced against Jordan.

Jordan may claim to be one of Great Britain's staunchest allies in the Near East, yet the attack on Jordan, the propaganda attack, has come from very unexpected quarters. The remarks on Jordan by Mr Tom Driberg, M.P., and other members of the Left-wing of the British Labour Party, suggesting that all British support for Jordan should be withdrawn, were much resented in Jordan; but perhaps the criticism that is still most resented was that contained in a series of talks on Israel and Jordan given by Mr Julian Duguid for the British Broadcasting Corporation.

When Mr Duguid applied for a Jordan visa he was told that the regulations made it impossible to grant a visa on a passport that bore an Israeli visa. The B.B.C. authorities then asked for special consideration—that the rule should be waived in Mr Duguid's case because "he is an acute and impartial observer for whom we have a great regard."

The Jordan Government responded to this plea by waiving the rules for Mr Duguid, and by making him welcome in Jordan. As they told me when I was in Amman, they would never have done this had not the B.B.C. been a British national institution.

They did not expect a pro-Jordanian picture, but they certainly did not expect what they got—a series of talks in which the poverty and "primitive" conditions of Jordan were held up to contrast with the civilization and delightful humanity of the young State of Israel.

There is also a source of angled news on Jordan with which the King has had to do battle through his Ambassadors. It is known in Jordan as the Beirut Hotel Bar dispatch. You may have noticed how many Press reports on the Near and Middle East have the date-line "Beirut." It is very natural. There is no more charming city between Paris and Singapore than the capital of the Lebanon. The superb view from my window there in the spring of 1959 showed the snow mountains rising to a sparkling blue sky on the right and an azure sea stretching to the left, making an unforgettable vista. Moreover, the city has everything: Arab hospitality, French culture—including French food, wines, and night clubs. There is no wonder that newspaper correspondents find it an attractive headquarters.

The city of Beirut is within a few flying hours of Damascus, Cairo, Baghdad, the Persian Gulf, Saudi Arabia, and, of course, Jerusalem and Amman. Unfortunately, the exciting event that hits the headlines has often happened while the reporter is still in Beirut—nothing then to be done but to send home the copy with the paradise date-line.

British and Jerusalem troops, June 7, 1958

128

The bagpipe band of the Jordan Army

Street scene, Amman

1

*The Dome of the Rock compound, and the steps down which Christ
drove the moneylenders*

A story that broke in this way was the story that King Hussein had "exiled" his brother, the Crown Prince Mohammed, because he had interfered in State affairs, and the Prime Minister, Majali, had protested against this. "The Crown Prince," the report stated, "was given an escort of Hunter jet fighters by the King to make it look as if his present trip was a normal visit."[1]

Any one who knows the character and inclinations of the King, of Majali, and of Prince Mohammed, would laugh at this fantastic story: but these facts are not available to the British readers. So two or three million readers get the impression of the utmost instability in Jordan, to the extent that the Hashemite House is divided against itself.

To counter the fitful world Press that Jordan had received since the Kingdom came into being, King Hussein, in his early days, could only meet and reassure the rulers who were, so to speak, on his doorstep, or whose Ambassadors were in Amman. He travelled for a day to the Saudi-Arabian border to meet King Saud. He had more than one meeting with the late King Faisal of Iraq. He sent messages of friendship to Britain, the United States, and Ankara; but it was clear that to establish Jordan's reputation as a progressive modern Arab state more was needed. In order to accomplish this the King embarked on his tour of 1959, the highlights of which were Washington and London.

This time the King did not fly out of Jordan through the Syrian air passage, where his plane had been shot at by United Arab Republic fighters the previous year. He

[1] Later the Crown Prince rejoined his brother in Amman.

left by going East, to Saudi Arabia, Pakistan, where the Moslem population gave him a rousing greeting—going East via Japan to the United States, and returning to Europe by London.

Press relations became an important factor of the King's tour, because the smaller embassies in Washington and London are not able to employ the expert public-relations staffs that more opulent missions can afford. This certainly applies to Jordan.

In the United States, although the King's reception was so cordial and his stay with the President most friendly, the more sensational newspapers were not able to resist the temptation of manufacturing a Royal romance. The young lady chosen for this fictitious rôle was unknown to the King, but this did not prevent photographs, purporting to show a romantic juxta-position, hitting the headlines.

The restraint of the British Press, however—not only the stuffier newspapers such as *The Times*, but the popular Press as well—always impresses foreigners. They suspect a secret censorship that does not exist. But there are ways of arranging these matters, up to a point, as we shall see later.

During the King's visit to London more than one newspaper was curious as to the present relationship between the King and Glubb Pasha, but both the King and General Glubb would only smile. Hussein has improved his technique of answering Press questions. He has adopted the plan that experienced politicians in-variably adopt—if the question can be answered they answer it directly. If it is a question they do not wish to answer they say something that they wish to say instead!

It is a brash reporter who points out that question and "answer" are unconnected!

After he had been President Eisenhower's guest for three days and had met, face to face, the dynamic, extrovert Press of America, the King received a wonderful accolade from the American newspapers. Almost without exception, they greeted him as a brave and independent young ruler battling against Communism, and striving to preserve the independence, faith, and culture of his Arab people.

In the meantime the King's Prime Minister, Samir Rifai, had carried on successful financial talks with the United States Treasury, and equally successful political talks with the State Department. The King's visit was in general and specific terms one of the most successful royal visits to Washington since the war.

Then, on Sunday, April 18, 1959, the King flew into London for ten days. Here he had very special problems to tackle. Leaving him in Amman three months earlier, I had asked, "Why do you not come and see us again in London?" The King smiled. "Yes, I think I may do that." He had, in fact, already planned his trip, but I think he was pleased that the question had been asked, for it showed that in the mind of the ordinary Englishman the strained relations that arose out of the dismissal of General Glubb were a thing of the past.

As indicated in Chapter 3, the King's visit to Britain was not a State visit. It was a private visit. He was not incognito. He came as King of Jordan, but he stayed privately at the Dorchester Hotel, in Park Lane, occupying with his entourage a suite on the first floor.

His reception by the Government, the Press, and the

people was obviously friendly, but, when the impact of his forthright personality began to make itself felt the Press gave him a more intimate and warmer welcome.

The British public responded to the appeal of the young King who was prepared to 'go it alone' if necessary. Very quickly, again with the able help of Mr Rifai, it was decided that the King would not have to 'go it alone.'

Within a week the British public was mildly surprised to learn that Britain was backing Jordan with funds, and the following day the public learnt that the United States and Britain had reached a gentlemen's agreement with Jordan.

Mr Samir Rifai, talking to me of this event, said, "Everything is all right now. Jordan is there to stay." There was no doubt in the mind of this astute politician, who started life as a clerk with the R.A.F., that the integrity of Jordan had become a major concern of the West.

Leading London newspapers told the story in their own way. The *Daily Mail*, under the heading, "We stand by Jordan with £2,500,000," said, "British policy in the Middle East is under urgent review. Quassem's lurch towards Communism in Iraq is now so pronounced that the old 'positions of strength' theories have to be revised. Long term guarantees for Jordan, which stand in the path of any Russian bid to dominate the Near East, may be necessary." Later in the same week the same paper stated that the Anglo-American agreement on Jordan was *un fait accompli*.

These remarkable financial and diplomatic victories would not have been possible had not the publics of

Britain and America adopted King Hussein as the young champion of a free way of life in the Near East. It was the impact of the King's vigorous and uncompromising personality that made itself felt.

The pattern of the King's visit to England followed an unconventional mould, dictated by the King's view of the people he wanted to see and thank. After lunching with the Queen at Windsor, he had long talks with the Prime Minister and Mr J. S. B. Lloyd. Then he went off to Aldershot to visit the 'Red Devils' who, as members of the parachute brigade, had dropped into Amman at the height of the Iraq Revolution.

This decision of the British Government, so vulnerable and so heavily attacked, especially by the Mikardo-type Member of Parliament and by the Soviet Press, turned out to be the one dramatic step that retrieved Britain's fortunes and good name in Jordan. Only one trick was missed—a joint march through Amman of the Jordan Army and their British guests before their departure.

The King spent a whole day and evening at Aldershot. The following day he was at Sandhurst. There he was received by General Urquhart, the commandant. As it happened, I had visited Sandhurst the previous week and had been most kindly received by the commandant and his officers. They had allowed me to check for myself the whole course of King Hussein's relations with Sandhurst.

I discovered that the King still had strong supporters, not only among the officers, but among the non-commissioned ranks. The King had passed out in six months instead of two years, for his majority was approaching and he had to return to Jordan. When, as

King, he did return to Sandhurst, he did not forget those who had helped him. To Regimental Sergeant-Major Lord he sent his signed photograph, now decorating the Lord house. "We had a great liking for him," said R.S.M. Lord. "He always had that quiet dignity that never deserted him."

But the King's visit was not all business. He visited the Haymarket Theatre to see Nigel Patrick and Coral Browne in *The Pleasure of his Company*, with the Duchess of Kent and Princess Alexandra. The same evening the King visited a famous London night club with another party, walking back to the Dorchester alone, and unguarded, in the early morning.

On the Wednesday of that week His Excellency Kasem Hashim, the urbane Jordanian Ambassador, gave a reception for the King at the Jordan Embassy, in Kensington Gardens—that same reception at which the meeting between the King and General Glubb, which I have described earlier, took place, and at which the British Cabinet was well represented.

As the King's visit drew to a close the public, as well as the Government, knew that a new era was being initiated in the Near East. They knew that this young visitor to Britain was important as representing the Arab viewpoint that did not wish to be dominated by any of the great Powers but was resolute in its opposition to the spread of agnostic, Communist influence.

Hussein has upheld his faith, for no other response would ever be possible for him. This sincerity had made itself felt. We are often prone to be critical of the Press in London, but in its understanding of the rôle that the King was playing, both the British and the American

Press showed understanding and sympathy. Had the Press attacked the new arrangements for Jordan— financial and political—it would have been much more difficult for an alternative Labour Foreign Secretary to honour the undertakings. As it is, they have found common consent, and only the quasi-Communist fellow-travellers in the House of Commons still carp at what has been done.

On the last day of the King's visit I asked him to give me a message for the British people. He did so. "I have been so happy to visit Britain again, and renew old friendships and familiar sights. The British people and Press have been very kind to me. I hope that before too long we will meet again. Please thank them for making me so welcome."

The simple words were printed. It was the end of a visit, in its way, without a rival. Twenty-four months before Britain and Jordan had had strained relations. The King had had to show the reason for his dismissal of Glubb Pasha. But Western political opinion was not slow to realize that the days were over when an Army could be commanded by seconded foreign officers. It soon rallied to the King's cause.

The King flew out of London. I went to see him off. He stood there, hatless, on the 'Tarmac,' waving to the Jordanian community who had come to bid him God-speed.

That evening he was in Rome, meeting the Italian President. Next day he was in Switzerland, then in Ankara; and within a week he was meeting the Shah, in Teheran, before the Persian King's State visit to London.

The meeting of the Shah and King Hussein had, for

me, a human interest. Both young men had been un-happy in the outcome of marriage. Both bore great responsibility. Both were being attacked by the Soviet radio and Press. Both were determined to retain the leadership of their nations.

Two days later the King was back on the small run-way of Amman airport. On the plane was General Sharrar, his Deputy Chief of Staff, who had accompanied him to London. It was said in London that the General belonged to the small clique of pro-Nasser officers who wished to reverse the foreign policy of Jordan. Next day the General was arrested at Army Headquarters and relieved of his command. I am convinced that should there be an attempted coup in Jordan it would be defeated in the first two vital hours if the King had a preconcerted plan to destroy it, over and above the usual police precautions for preventing treason.

My long experience of Eastern revolution had taught me the truth of this. But the King has one asset even more vital and disconcerting to his enemies: he has a sure instinct that tells him who his friends are—and who are his enemies.

A Near-Eastern ruler needs instinct as well as judgment.

13
"They shall be one People"

To bring the picture of King Hussein of Jordan into true perspective, we must always remember the stage on which the action of Hussein's life takes place. It is a colourful, but ever-changing scene. The rare air of Amman enables the people of Amman to work far harder than the clotted, suffocating atmosphere of Baghdad in the hot weather allows. The Jordanian is a vital, active person, quick to laughter and tears.

It is a scene in which great wealth now begins to appear side by side with poverty. Cadillacs as well as camels block the narrow streets of the capital. There is at least the danger of an impression that has, in the past, proved fatal to many political societies—irresponsible wealth and irresponsible violence. This is an aspect of Jordanian life that the King has to watch constantly. Finally, it is a scene in which the Army and the Police play a large rôle. In the years of stress that have recently passed this was unavoidable, but in the new era which has commenced for Jordan it should become less necessary.

The King's actions and his reactions are only explicable if this background is understood. There is still a feeling of claustrophobia in Jordan. The Government are still very careful about allowing Jordanians to travel out of Jordan. The aftermath of crisis still hangs heavy in the air; but it is lifting. Each month that passes shows an improvement in the situation, new friendships formed abroad, old enmities healed, the number of political prisoners reduced. It has been an epic struggle, and its effect on the King's character will last as long as he lives.

The King has grown in stature and self-reliance. I think his tour in the summer of 1959 played a part in this. Hussein has always combined a shy, and even retiring, personality with great political toughness. Perhaps now he is less shy than he was. He certainly appears to be. His courtesy and kindness remain as they have always been, and there are many stories told in Jordan which illustrate these pleasing traits in the King's character.

When motoring in the country he will give a lift to young soldiers trudging for miles in the heat to reach their homes in time for a week-end leave. The excitement as the King's car draws up to the little house can well be imagined.

His concern for the half million refugees in Jordan is constant and practical. He is always thinking of new ways in which the lives they lead can be made more bearable, even more enjoyable. The King has one trait that has earned him many dividends. He is no snob. He treats all men as equals, not as a matter of policy, but because he feels that way about them.

In his visits to America and Britain he answered the American and British reporters quietly and with obvious conviction. He put on no 'airs.' This endeared him to the tough, restless men who work for the newspapers. The King was very well reported.

While he was in the States, the King met the

uninhibited bombardment of the Press with a smile, as part of the brash, warm welcome he received from the American people. The King made friends with the President. The old soldier and the soldierly young King seemed to take to each other, and understand each other, from the start.

In Britain His Excellency the Jordanian Ambassador, who, if one may say so without disrespect, "knows all the answers," determined to avoid a repetition of the New York incident, wrote an admirable letter to the Newspaper Proprietors' Association which was posted in the News Rooms of the great London Dailies.

Incidentally, thereby hangs a tale. The Ambassador's original and natural idea was to forward his letter through the Foreign Office. Asking me what I thought of the plan, I replied, "If it comes from the Foreign Office the Press may ignore it, as they don't like Government interference; but if it comes from you personally, as you are our guest here, they will treat it with consideration."

The Ambassador saw the point in a flash. "Ah, yes!" he said. "In Britain . . ."

The result was that the King was free to travel anywhere in Britain without too much Press pressure, and he was allowed to relax and enjoy himself in peace.

The King's peace, however, was soon to be broken. He and his entourage occupied a suite on the first floor of the Dorchester Hotel. General Sharrar was there. The Prime Minister, Mr Samir Rifai, having completed very successful meetings in Washington and London, was about to resign, and Haaza Pasha Majali, also with the King, was about to succeed Rifai. General Sharrar was to be relieved of his position and placed under house arrest. A drama was certainly in progress on the first floor of the Dorchester. Akef Faiz, son of Sheik Mithcal Faiz, was the only constant factor—he was to remain Minister of Agriculture.

Samir Rifai had been very successful as Prime Minister, dragging Jordan back from the brink of disaster, in 1957, to stability and peace. His foreign mission in the United States and Britain put Jordan on an entirely new footing, virtually guaranteed by the great Western Powers. Why, then, did he resign? The official communiqué said that Mr Rifai had resigned for health reasons, but this was, I feel, Arab courtesy, and was not intended to be seriously believed.

In fact, the King and Mr Rifai took different views as to how to cope with the struggle for power going on in the Jordan Army; a matter which included Sharrar's arrest. So King and Prime Minister decided that a change would be a good thing. They remain the best of friends.

Haaza Pasha Majali, the new Prime Minister—and Foreign Minister—is, surely, one of the most outspoken Arab leaders on the international stage. "I just say what I think," says this remarkable man. "People know this, so they don't take offence."

Having adopted this technique, novel for an Eastern courtier and politician, the Prime Minister, who is regarded as strongly realistic in his policies, says exactly what is in his mind, whether it is acceptable or not.

The stern hand that Mr Rifai had had to use to bring Jordan through the crisis that followed the 1956 elections and the Iraq Revolution made him some enemies. Now, in retirement, he has well-deserved leisure, and the people will have time to reflect coolly on what might have happened if there had been no Samir Rifai to support and aid the young King.

Out, with Mr Rifai, went the Rifai Cabinet. In came a new set of Ministers. We may mention the chief Ministers: Mr Rifai had kept the portfolios of the Premiership, Foreign Affairs, and Defence in his own strong hands. The new Prime Minister has retained the first two, but nominated Anwar Nafhashibi as his Minister of Defence. Key-man in the Cabinet is Khulusi Khiry, the Minister of Economic Affairs. The Sheikh Mohammed Amen Shankati became Minister of Education.

The Cabinet gives the impression of working as a team under the King for objectives similar to those pursued by Samir Rifai. So, without any change in its declared foreign policy, a new team took over in Jordan, guided, as before, by the King—but a more mature, stronger King.

Those close to the King have been convinced during the last two years that he is not influenced in his politics by any one, though listening attentively to all advice. His relations with Queen Zayn remain unchanged, but he is a man now, and a man hardened and steeled in a stern school.

The King was, of course, asked about possible marriage plans when he was abroad. A bachelor King is a provocation to the journalists, who love nothing more than to report a romance—and a wedding: the human story. Would the King choose an Islamic bride? Was he attached to the Princess Huzina? When would he marry? To all questions the King gave the same reply: "I have so much to do. It is too early to think of marriage." And no farther could the diligent reporters get.

Having watched the Jordan scene so closely, I feel that the interest now lies in two directions:

First, can the crisis in Jordan be completely overcome? This, I think, resolves itself into the protection of the King. As long as the King is there, Jordan will come through.

In a state such as Jordan, where there is explosive, hidden political material, it is necessary not only to take the usual precautions against sedition, but to have a preconceived plan, instantly capable of being operated, which can be put into action in the event of an attempt to seize power by ambitious public men. Having seen five revolutions myself, I know that success depends on the element of surprise in the first hour. If the revolutionaries are themselves surprised by the quick unfolding of a counterplan of which they have had no knowledge, the revolt fails.

The dedicated General Tabbara, Director-General of Police in Amman, looks after the first precaution. The second is a matter for the highest authority to perfect in the greatest detail. The awful murders of Baghdad, which outraged the people of Iraq and shocked the world, must at all costs be prevented from any repetition in Amman.

The second, and equally important feature of the future that now opens up before us, is the King's ability, not only to rule, but to lead on to better and broader ways of life. Elections are due in Jordan, and I believe that political parties will not be allowed to resume activities before they take place, after the disasters that followed the 1956 elections; but private citizens will stand for the fifty seats of the new Parliament[1]—and no doubt friends of the same persuasion will work together.

These are the changes and trends in Jordan. We are leaving the scene dominated by the King to a greater extent than before, a King confident in his mission, determined to bring success, peace, and prosperity to the Jordan people.

If the battle is won, as we may pray and believe it will be, it will be fair to say that never has a young nation owed more to one man.

[1] The number of seats was increased from forty to fifty in 1957.

14
The King's Destiny

I have attempted in this biography to paint a true picture of King Hussein. Although I see him as a brave and dedicated young man, I have not gone out of my way to ascribe to him virtues or gifts that he does not possess, nor have I dug into his personal life to reveal intimacies to satisfy sensation-seeking readers. I hold that this King's story is vivid and interesting enough as it stands.

The story of Hussein is essentially a human story, and I have tried to tell it in simple terms. I wanted to write the whole truth as it really happened and as it is, from day to day, enacted by the King and his Ministers, in Amman.

As I come to the end of the portrait one question above all others seeks to be answered. Millions of people, were they to read this story, either in its present form or serialized in a newspaper, would say: "Yes, indeed he is a young man of courage and singleness of purpose, but has not this kind of leadership had its day? Does anyone really want kings any more, and the things that kings stand for?" Unless we can answer that question clearly and convincingly, then King Hussein's kind of leadership is doomed, if not now, in the not too distant future.

I have lived for a quarter of a century in the East, and have seen the awakening of the Eastern nations from their long periods of British, French, and Dutch domination. It has been made very clear to me that democracy, as we understand it, has very little chance of substituting the old colonial rule without dynamic and respected leadership from above. The man who, alone, can give this type of leadership in an Eastern state is the King. This applies to the Near East just as forcefully as it does to the Far East. It may not apply with equal force to India, where political tutelage and development was, and is, of a very high order, though I think I could make a case of Mr Nehru having, in effect, been the Emperor of India, since Independence. He is a high-caste Hindu, and has several kingly attributes.

In Jordan the position is clearer, more urgent. There is no one in Jordan who can lead the nation as the King can lead it. The future lies in the direction in which the King can guide his people; and this is the crux of the Hussein story. Can the King, now that order and security have been restored in Jordan, himself initiate a more liberal and democratic regime without the terrible repercussions that upset Jordan and the whole Near East in the crisis period of 1956 and 1957?

I believe he can, and will, do this.

The weapons with which the King fights for what he believes to be right are powerful weapons. First, and foremost, there is his courage and absolute dedication to the cause of Jordan and her people. Secondly, there is his heritage as a descendent of the Prophet. He is a good Moslem, which makes him a natural protector of Islam. Thirdly, there is his natural aptitude for Eastern politics, his ability to see right through complicated questions and tear out the heart of the question.

Finally, the King has good friends. I do not refer only to the unpublished agreement, already noted, with America and Britain. I refer also to the King's close neighbours. The Government of the Lebanon has always treated the Hashemite House with courtesy and regard. The Saudi-Arabian Government look on the King as an Arab Prince with the closest ties uniting him to them. Even President Nasser, who, six months ago, allowed Radio Cairo to attack King Hussein day and night, has changed his mind—he is no longer an enemy, but not yet a friend.

How could the King begin to initiate a new Jordan, not the crisis-packed country of latter years, but a new well-balanced State?

The dual aim of his policy must be to rid himself at the earliest possible moment of reliance on foreign aid—American or British. The future of Jordan lies within, not without, the Arab brotherhood. Apart from the discovery of oil, this can only be achieved by an agricultural revolution in which more modern methods are employed and production greatly stimulated. The Army must be kept out of politics, and, in order to achieve this, the rates of pay of all ranks must be adequate. Social reform in health, housing, old age, and a multitude of other matters must engage the King's attention. In order to achieve all this he must win the regard and affection of the potential political leaders. In great measure he has this already, but the palace has yet to become identified with progress in the minds of the people.

I have used the imperative phrase here because the King himself is very much aware of a second phase now opening in Jordan. Up to now it has been a battle for survival. Was King Hussein to win—or was Jordan to go the way of Iraq? This has been the one and only issue. Now a new set of objectives springs on to the national map.

Undoubtedly the rôle of Arab leadership is vacant at the moment. President Nasser looked like taking it at one time. In his own words, he appeared to be the actor who could fill the rôle that was crying to be played. Nasser saw very clearly that only Arab nationalism could keep Communism out of the vacuum caused by the end of Anglo-French Near-Eastern dominion, but his decisions, his speeches, and his foreign policy are altogether unpredictable. They compare very unfavourably with the constancy of King Hussein. It looks now as if Hussein, not Nasser, is the stuff of which true leaders are made, for resolution is the basis of leadership. Where there is no vision the people perish.

Extremist politicians in Jordan like to portray the King as being subject to the constant pressure of the American and British Ambassadors carrying out the instructions of their respective Governments, but even they themselves do not believe this is true. The Jordan people know their King, and they recognize that in this young man they have as their leader a remarkably independent person. Hussein's strength lies in the fact that he is a true Jordanian, and the people know this.

The fact that he is not fanatical is fast becoming a help instead of a hindrance, for education and foreign contacts by Press and radio are transforming the people of Jordan. They know that under their King they have the opportunity of playing an honourable and free rôle in world affairs, beholden to no nation, but in close concert with the Arab sister states. The Jordan public are growing up, and, as they do so, the old type of pseudo-fanatic, quasi-religious leader asserts less and less influence. The people realize that the King is educated, balanced, and faithful. That is all they ask.

In the Near East kingship is on trial. In Europe we know that the most advanced and democratic states—Britain, Sweden, Denmark, Norway, and Belgium—have kingly Governments, and that their monarchies play a great part in preserving the balance of party battle, and the underlying decencies that rule public and private life. But in the Near East kingship is challenged largely because the present dynasties are mainly descended from Arab princes who found favour with the former colonial or mandatory Powers.

As soon as Eastern kingship can take one giant step forward and release itself from the past to grip the leadership of the future it will have no rival in the Arab countries. The restoration of a king in both Egypt and Iraq is by no means a wild dream. The chaotic situation in Iraq in particular has made millions secretly yearn for a return of the monarchy, but in a more modern form than it assumed under the rule of Nuri Said.

To all these influences King Hussein is intensely alive. He must lead and not be led. This he knows.

The alternative to constitutional monarchy in the Near East is not radical democracy. The alternative is Communism or military dictatorship, which may or may not be able to tolerate some form of subject parliamentary government.

President Nasser has been able to promulgate a new Constitution, but General Quassem has had to insist that virtually all civil liberties and, of course, political parties, should be suspended.

The rôle that the Army is to play in the future of Jordan is of paramount importance. If they can stay with the American, British, or, for that matter, the Russian pattern of non-interference in politics, Jordan has great hope. But if the Army is tempted to intervene in every crisis, and even to take to itself more and more power, then the unfortunate pattern of South America and the Far East might well become the pattern in the Near East too.

The habit of the swift, silent coup is a bad habit, and it is a habit that may become an addiction. The Jordan Army, in its tradition of loyalty to its Commander-in-Chief, sets an example to the new Near-Eastern states.

We live in a tense, restless world, where great new forces are doing battle. In this giant struggle the Near-Eastern nations appear to be but little concerned. Their immediate anxiety is to mould the resurgent Arab movement along paths that will bring prosperity to the Arab peoples. Only if action is taken to solve the Israeli-Arab dispute in the very near future will the leaders be able to bring peace as well as prosperity to their people.

If, as we hope, the Arab-Israeli dispute is settled without bloodshed, the future of Jordan, after five years of struggle, is brighter. Her own resources in minerals alone have not seriously been developed. For many years they were deliberately hidden. Her international relationships continue to improve. Her domestic economy begins to expand. The national spirit of the Jordanian people begins to rally behind their King.

In America and Britain we should not measure the success of Hussein and his policies by estimating to what extent they promote our interests, nor should we hide our own interest in oil and trading under such phrases as "Near-Eastern peace," "Stability in the Middle East," and others, to cloak our 'vital' interests in this area.

We must face firmly the fact that the time is fast approaching when all the wealth of the Near East, discovered and undiscovered, will be firmly in the hands of the new nations concerned.

In particular, British and American oil interests will have to give the major profit, from well to pump, to the owning governments—or quit the Near East for good.

It is extraordinarily difficult for Western observers, politicians in particular, to realize that the Near and Middle East is no longer, in any sense, a sphere of influence. In Jordan, as in the Lebanon and the United Arab Republic, there is still much friendship for the West, but there is universal dislike and distrust of Anglo-American oil politics.

There is one other factor in East-West relationships that is in a state of flux. The image of the Near-Eastern nations that we have in the West is a distorted one, a decade out of date. Arab nationalism, robust, intolerant, sensitive, has come to stay. Its more urbane manifestation may not be long delayed. The basic truth is this—that all men cherish freedom. Russian aid, American aid, British aid, are all unwelcome if they mean that freedom suffers; but the help that a powerful friend freely gives his neighbour is welcomed gratefully, as a gesture between free men.

To understand King Hussein we have to be willing to

meet his Arab people as they really are, not as we would have them to be.

The phase when Jordan needs financial aid may well pass, but her need for understanding will continue. Her problems and her people are in many ways unique, but they are so important to us that we should all try to understand the Jordanian way of life.

That way of life is the way the Prophet revealed fifteen centuries ago. It is that way of life which Hussein of Jordan fights daily to preserve.

15

Hussein in the New Decade

In the winter of 1959 King Hussein left Jordan on a working holiday, visiting Switzerland, Germany, and Britain. The visit to Britain was remarkable, for during his three-week stay in London the King, on his own initiative, commenced to trace a pattern of kingship which neither the East nor the West had ever seen before.

He adopted complete informality in his day-to-day contacts. He turned from great affairs to small cases of individual hardship, such as meeting the expense of a small Arab boy who would lose his sight unless he could be operated on by the world's best surgeons; and he seemed determined to follow up the political achievements of his June visit to the United States and Britain by making informal and friendly contact with the people.

Within six hours of arriving in London he appeared in the B.B.C. programme *This is Your Life*, in which Eamonn Andrews depicted the career of Regimental Sergeant-major Lord. Just before leaving, on January 1, 1960, the King appeared in the searching programme *Face to Face*, answering all the questions that John Freeman had prepared to reveal the King's real character and intentions.

In this way Hussein made his impact on millions, and achieved his objective of putting the image of modern kingship across to a very large public. He went a great deal further in democratic public relations than our own Royal family have yet been permitted to do; only Prince Philip—appearing in the not too heavy disguise of a scientist—has initiated a similar approach.

The curious fact is that the remarkable innovations of King Hussein on television may be said to be in the old tradition of Arab princes and leaders. In the Near East the personal impact of the ruler was always what counted. If the nation accepted the leader as their man his cause was their cause, to death. Hussein seems to know that it is on this personal impact that the future of kings as leaders rests. It is a remarkable achievement and indicates clear vision. To break into the public relations of so traditional a country as Britain with a novel approach and a completely fresh impact shows originality, a quality which the King has added to his courage.

The King's television appearances were gripping. This was his description of the assassination of his grandfather, in the Temple of the Rock, in Jerusalem:

"I was about three paces behind my grandfather when we entered the gate, and, suddenly, I saw some one rush from a door to the right side with a revolver in his hand, and before any one could do anything he fired a shot. My grandfather was hit, and fell. I received a bullet that ripped a medal off my chest."

The King's personal revelation was candid. He had a job to do, he said, a job he must complete, but, "I wish that I could be a normal person in a strong, free Arab world that is united and progressive, rather than be the King of a small country where I might be an obstruction to unity."

The King pointed plainly to the path he wishes to

pursue. The reopening of diplomatic relations with Egypt is the first overt step to ensure eventual Arab solidarity. The next step, although this has not yet been suggested even in the Press in the West or the Near East, will undoubtedly be a settlement of the Israeli dispute, that includes the burning question of the Arab refugees.

Arab-Israeli relationships are changing under the surface. The Israeli Government has already agreed to compensation in principle, "even if it takes us twenty years to regain our loss." Incidents on the Jordan-Israeli border have been growing fewer yearly, and the many miles of unguarded desert border between the nations has not been violated. The truth is that King Hussein, with the other Arab leaders, faces the fact that the West—in particular, America and Britain—will not allow the destruction of the State of Israel.

For the first time Arab leaders are, unofficially, acknowledging that there is a State of Israel, not merely 'Jewish-occupied territory.' Arab-Israeli peace to supplant the present armistice is not far ahead. As King Hussein has the longest border with Israel—and the best-disciplined Army in the Near East—it is inevitable that he will take a leading part in the establishment of peace in the Near East in the immediate future.

Once again we will find that this young man is a step ahead of contemporary thought and policies. As he strides into the new decade, with all its dangers and great opportunities, we may well salute him, for on the growth of his character and wisdom great issues depend.

Note

The assassination of Premier Haaza Pasha Majali, in August 1960, while he was working in the Prime Minister's room at the Foreign Office in Amman, by means of time-bombs planted in the building appeared to end, for a time, the period of comparative tranquillity that Jordan was beginning to enjoy.

King Hussein at once accused persons resident in the United Arab Republic of being the instigators of this terrible murder, in which ten other persons lost their lives.

The King, with characteristic courage, attended the funeral of his friend and faithful servant. The late Premier, a member of a powerful bedouin family, strongly favoured Jordan's friendship with her Western allies.

Strict security measures were at once imposed in Amman, and a huge gathering of the public mourned the victims of this outrage, which had the effect of further uniting the King and his people.

Index

INDEX